ヒコウキ

AIRPLANE
(Hikoki)

Once you've made the airplane, fly it! As shown in the photo, hold the bottom of the airplane, keep it level, and push it forward to give it momentum, then release. Try flying it from high places or compete to see who can fly their plane the highest.

TEAR OFF COLORED SHEET ALONG THIS EDGE

1

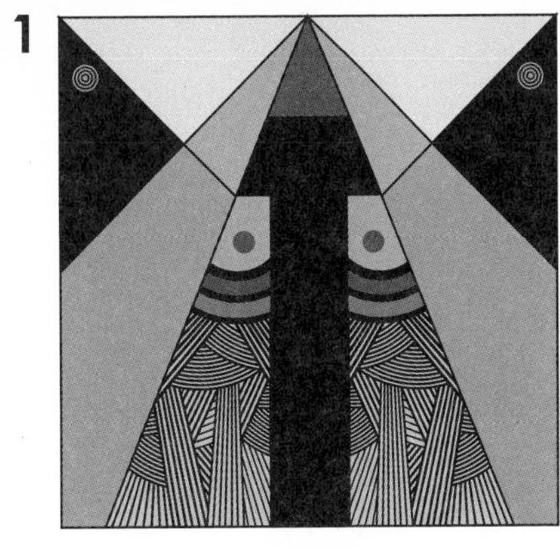

Turn over.

2

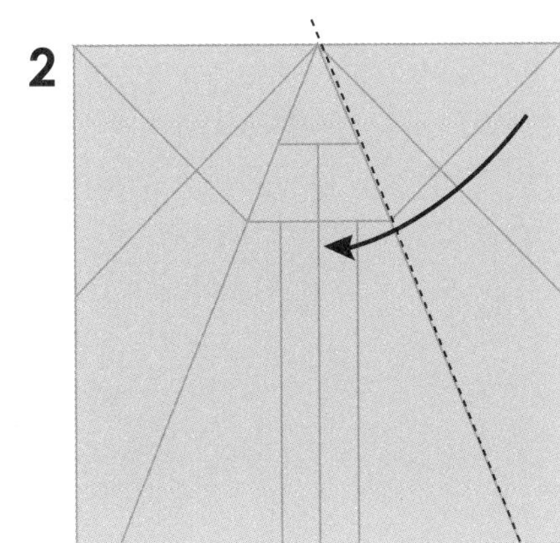

TEAR OFF COLORED SHEET ALONG THIS EDGE

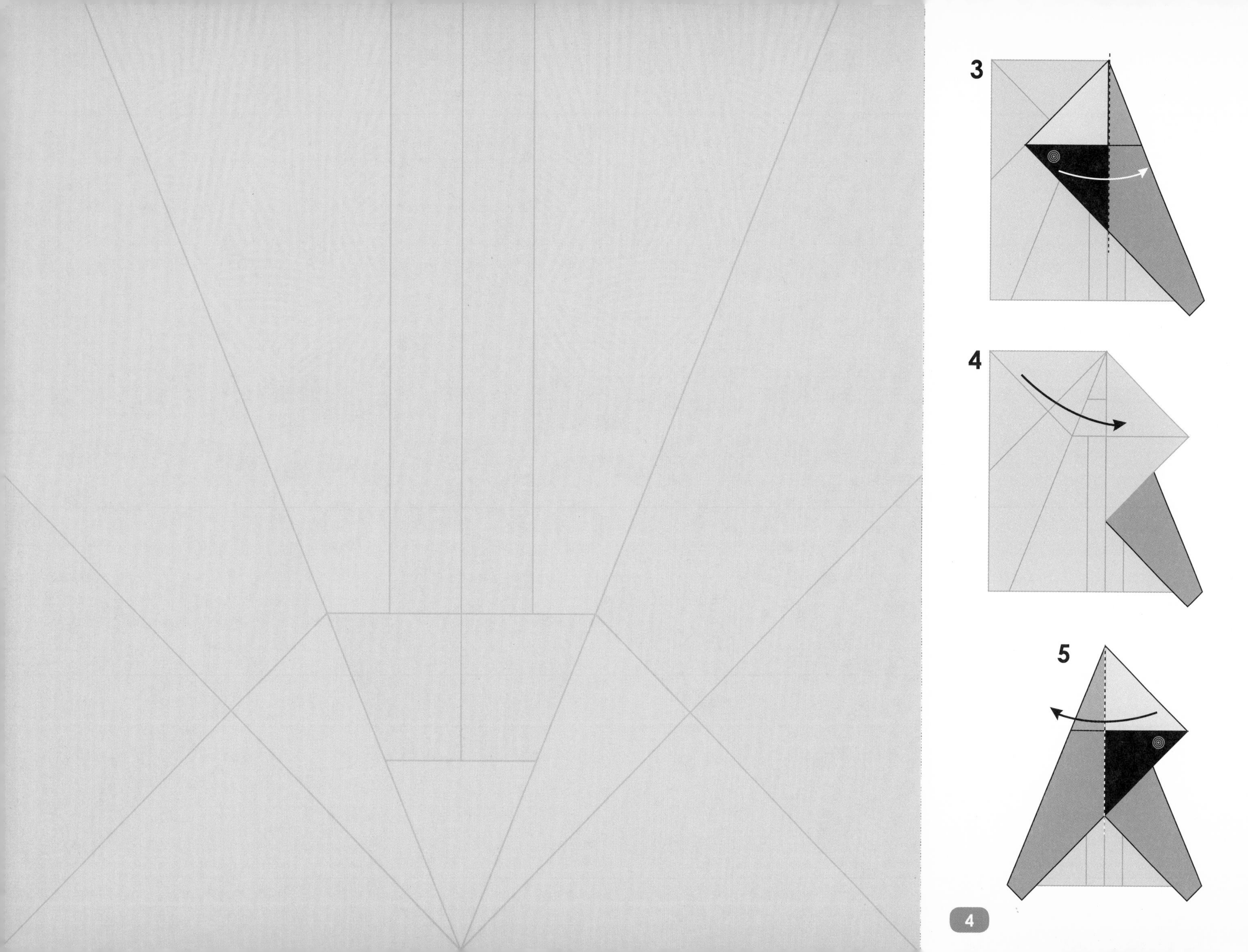
3
4
5

6

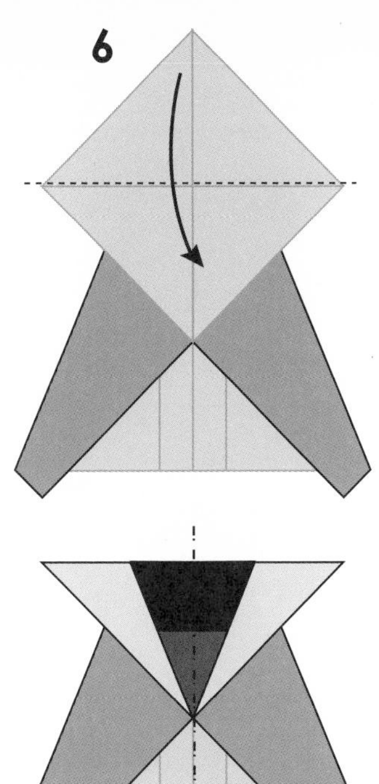

7

Mountain fold in half.

8

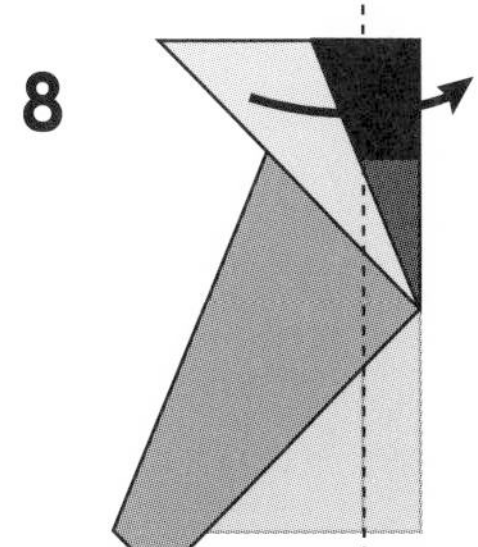

Valley fold to spread the wing. Do the same on the reverse.

TEAR OFF COLORED SHEET ALONG THIS EDGE

9

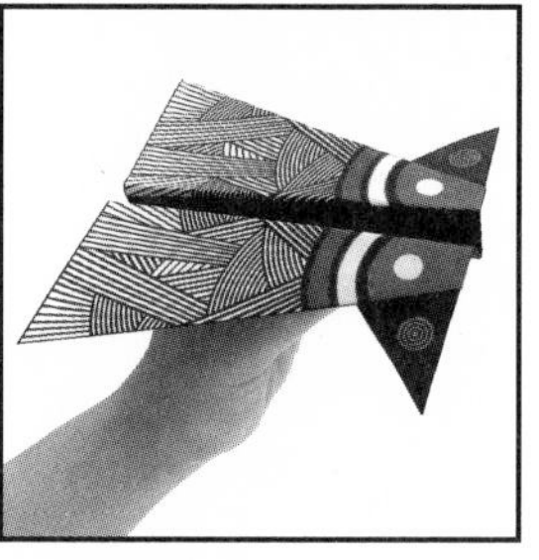

Hold from the bottom and let fly!

ヤマタニオバケ

BELLOWS
(Yamatani-obake)

At first, it's just a bunch of circles, but when you expand the pleats, out comes an alien! It's great for playing Peek-a-Boo with babies. Why not draw your own pictures and create an original card? Just match up and fold the horizontal lines accordion-style.

TEAR OFF COLORED SHEET ALONG THIS EDGE

Mountain fold=MF Valley fold=VF

1

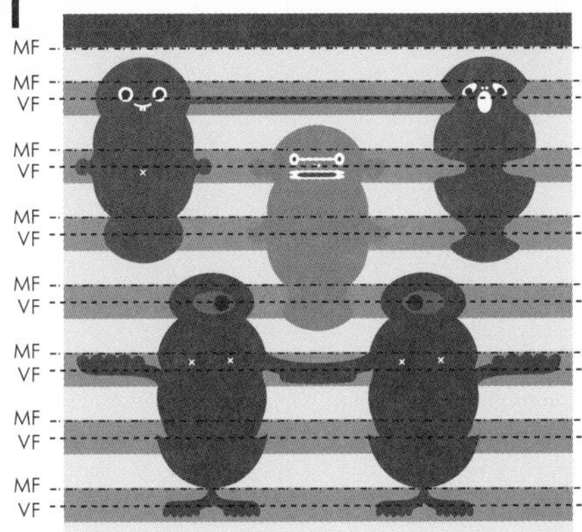

2

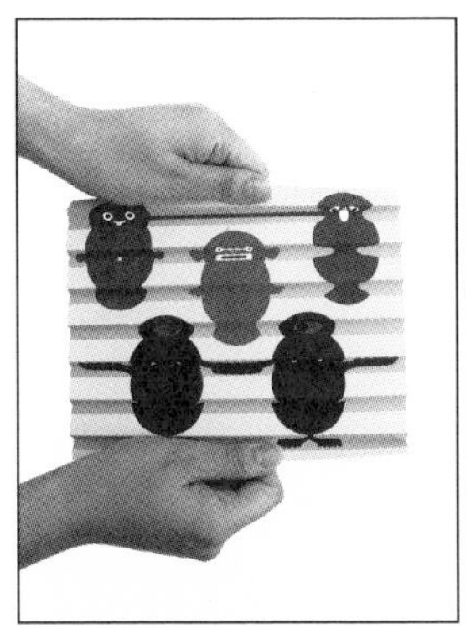

Pleat with alternate mountain and valley folds so that only the paler-colored portions are visible. When you spread the paper and open the pleats, ETs appear!

TEAR OFF COLORED SHEET ALONG THIS EDGE

TEAR OFF COLORED SHEET ALONG THIS EDGE

ハコ

BOX
(Hako)

From a single piece of paper comes a cute little box. Fill it with candy or marshmallows and give it as a present! Of course, it can also be used as a pouch for holding knick-knacks. Also try using a larger piece of paper or paper with your favorite design to create a whole new box.

TEAR OFF COLORED SHEET ALONG THIS EDGE

TEAR OFF COLORED SHEET ALONG THIS EDGE

4

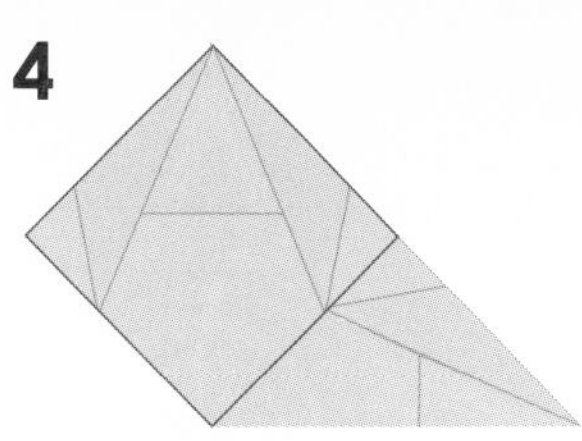

Turn over.

5

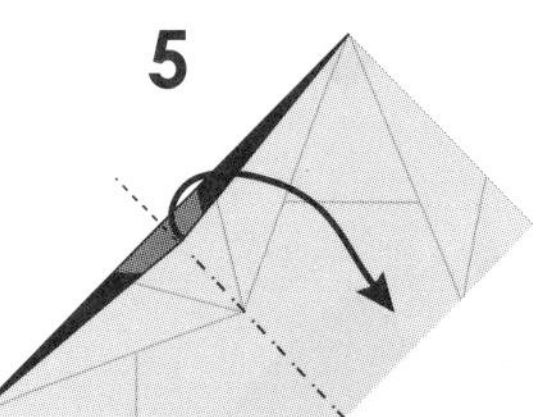

Spread as you lift open at the edge and press down flat.

6

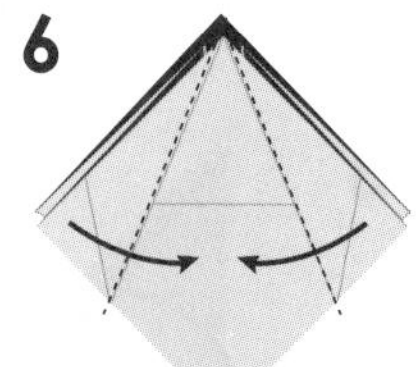

7

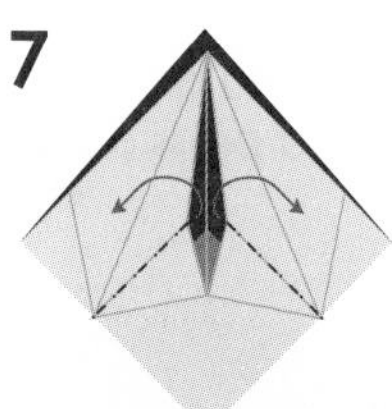

Spread as you lift open at the edge and press down flat.

8

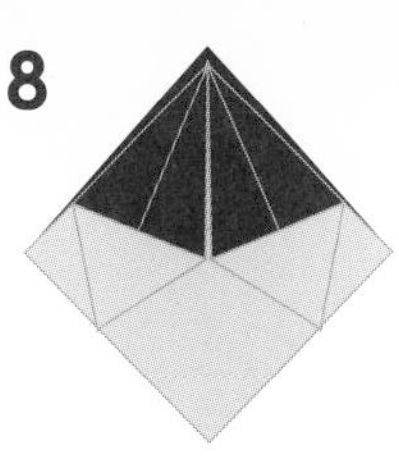

As you did in step 7, spread as you lift open at the edge and press down flat.

9

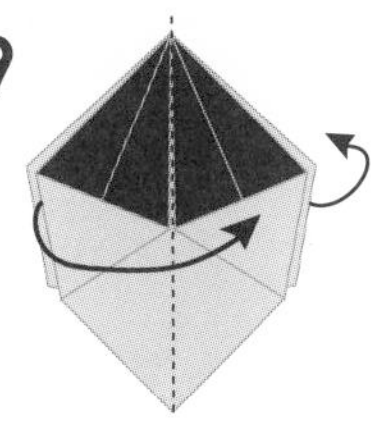

Turn one layer to expose the layer on the reverse.

10

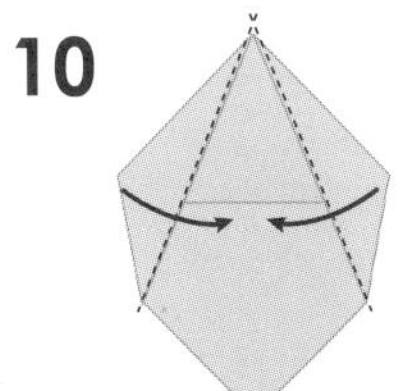

11

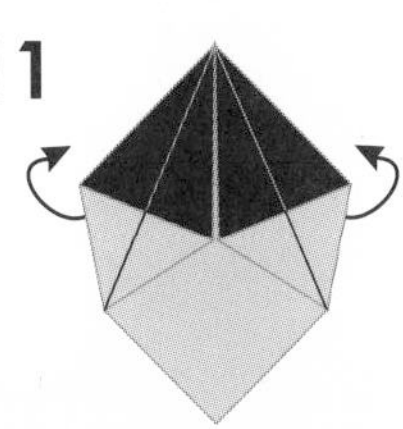

Do the same on the opposite side.

TEAR OFF COLORED SHEET ALONG THIS EDGE

12

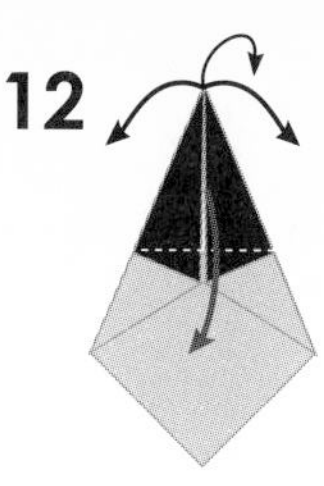

Fold down all 4 corners.

13

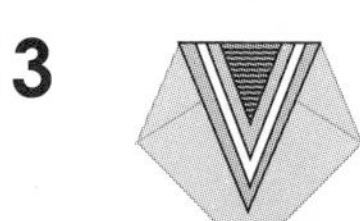

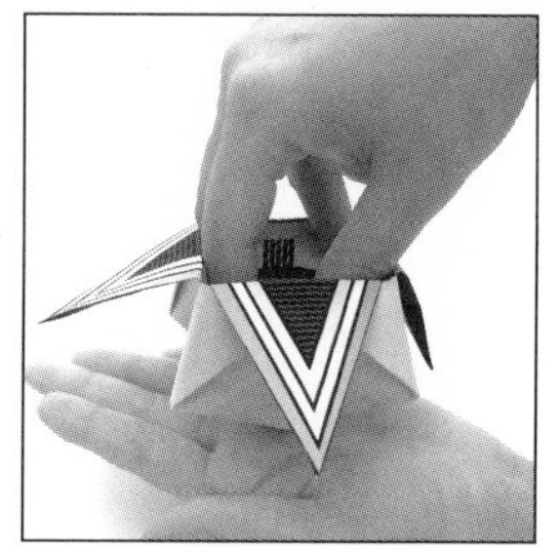

Insert your fingers and spread open the interior until the bottom is completely flat.

カメラ

CAMERA
(Kamera)

Holding the "camera" as shown in the photo, pull on the flaps and the shutter will "click" open! Have fun making a personalized camera by sticking a portrait or photo on the "cochae" part. It's great for presenting a surprise message to a friend.

TEAR OFF COLORED SHEET ALONG THIS EDGE

cochae

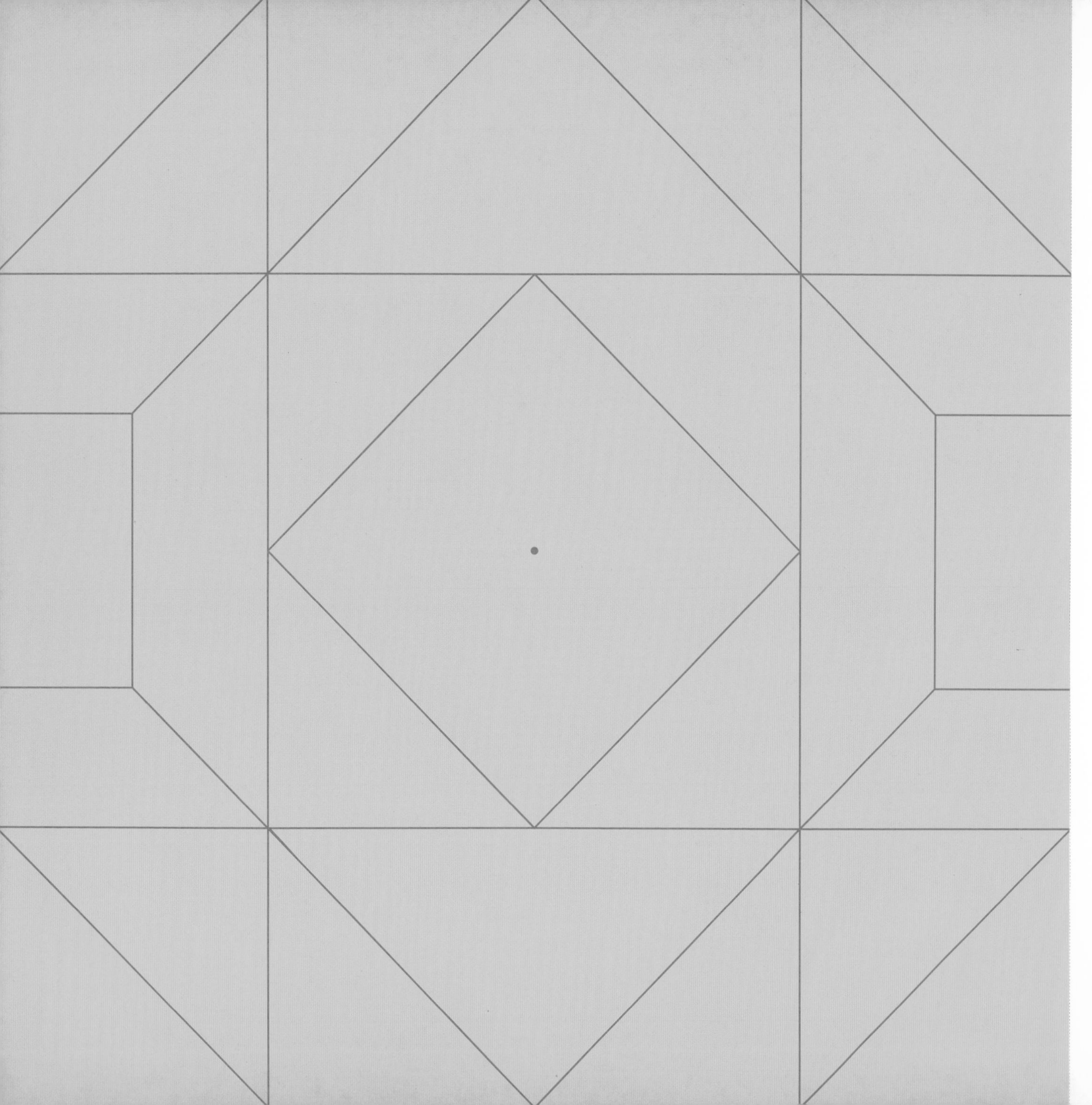

1

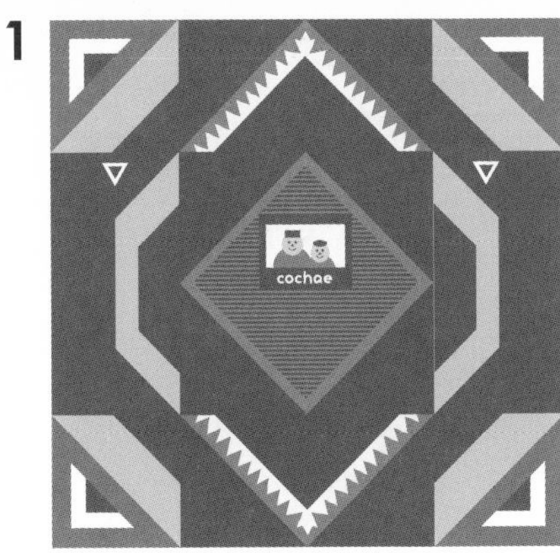

Turn over.

2

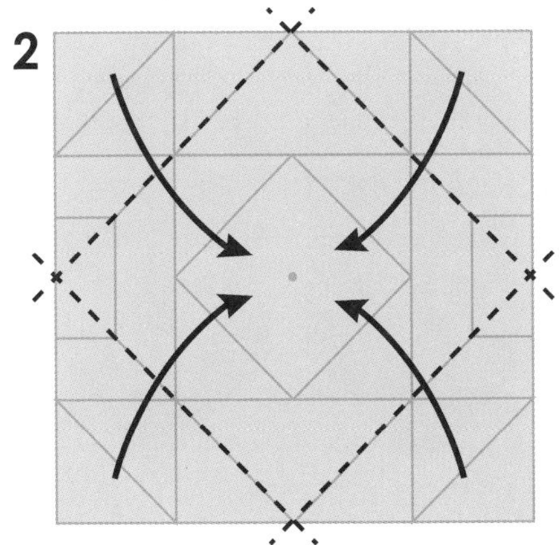

Fold in all four corners to meet in the center.

TEAR OFF COLORED SHEET ALONG THIS EDGE

cochae

3

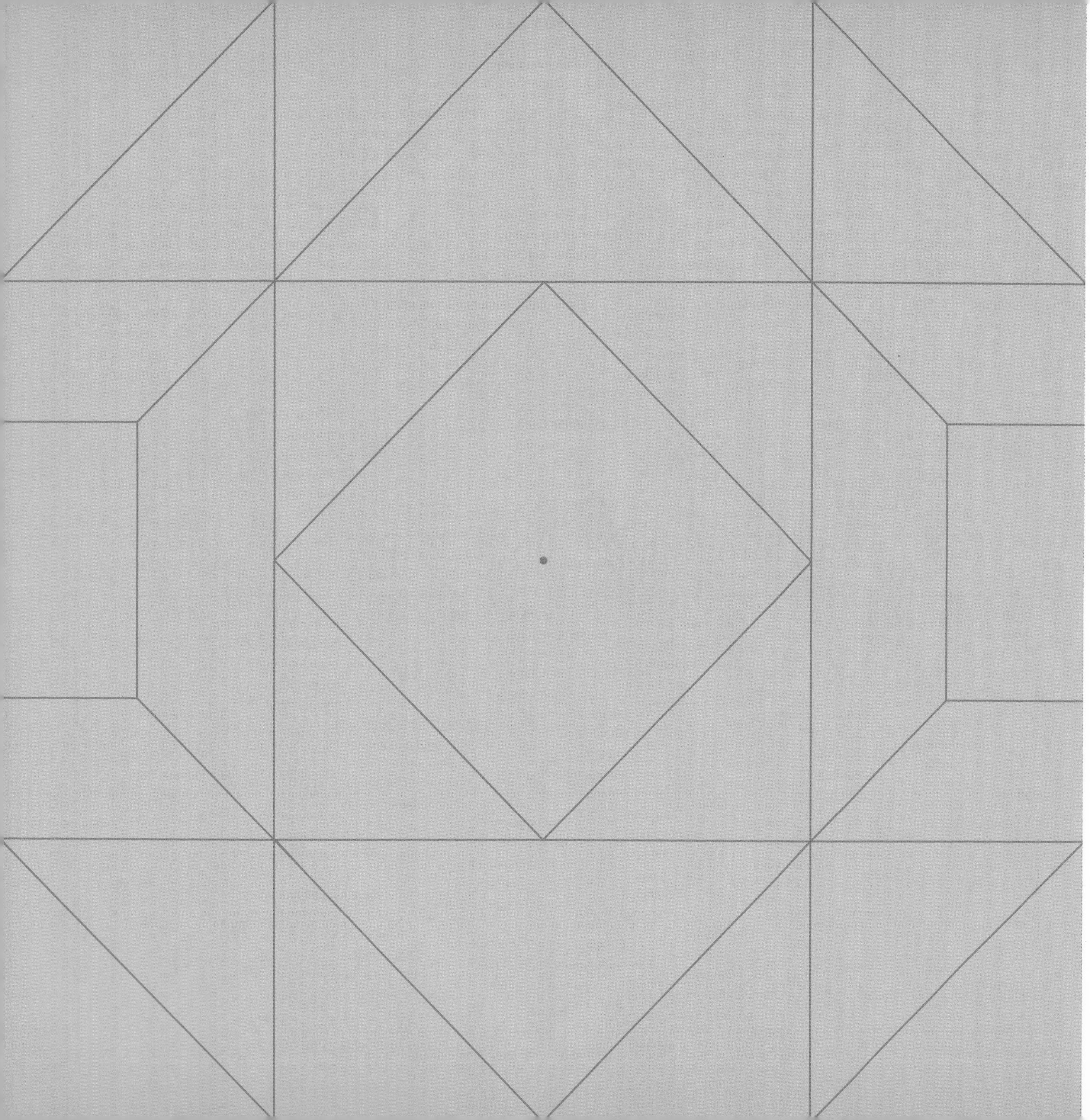

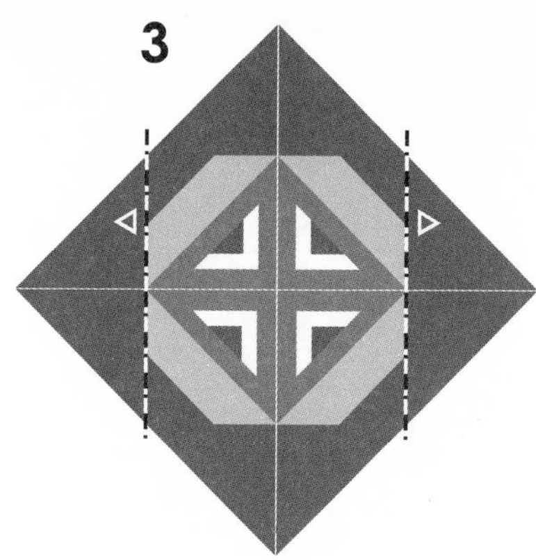

Mountain fold on the reverse.

4

5

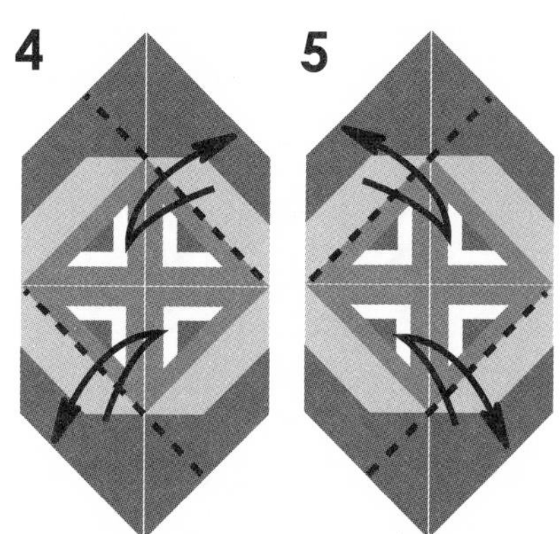

Make creases as shown.

6

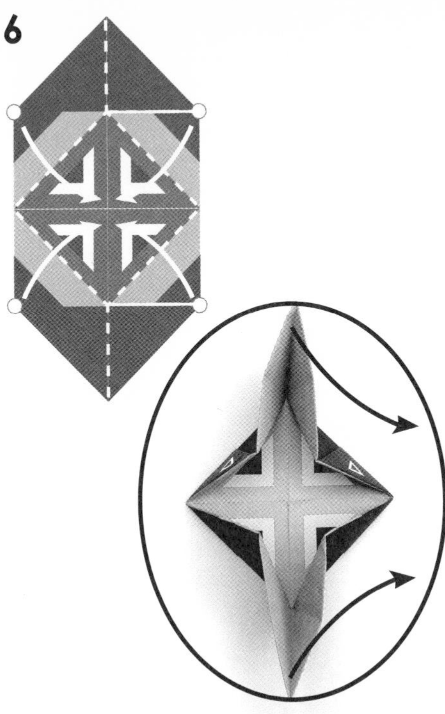

Using the creases as a guide, pinch and lift up at the circled points and fold the corners outward and to the right as shown. Pay attention to the mountain-and valley-fold markings. See process photo.

7

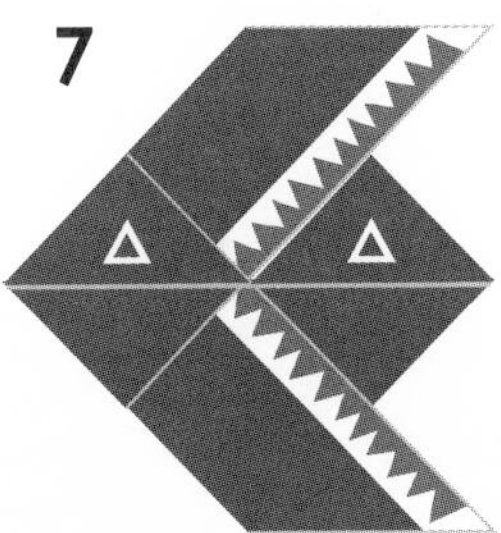

The piece should look like this.

Turn over.

TEAR OFF COLORED SHEET ALONG THIS EDGE

cochae

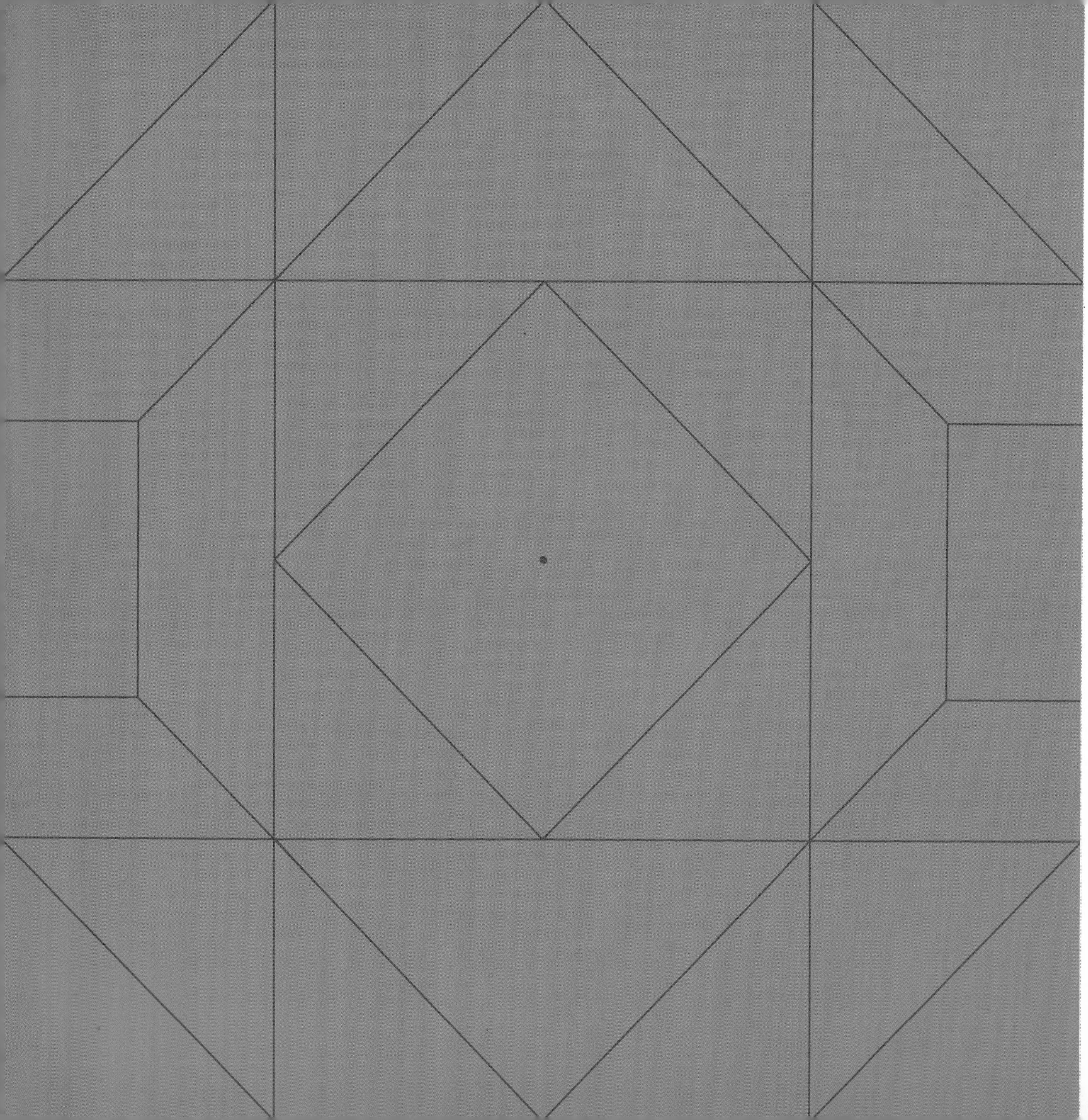

8

Spread as you lift open the inside corners and press down flat.

9

Turn over.

10

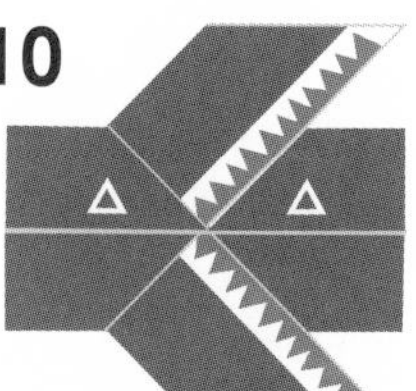

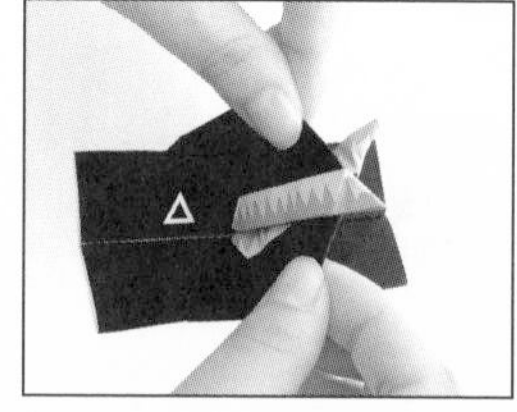

Bring the top and bottom pointed edges together and fold over the ends to hold in place.

コップ

DRINKING CUP
(Koppu)

Press both sides toward the center, to pop the cup open. What could go inside? If you make the cup with sturdy paper, you can even pour in water, which will surprise the kids! Be sure to try it out.

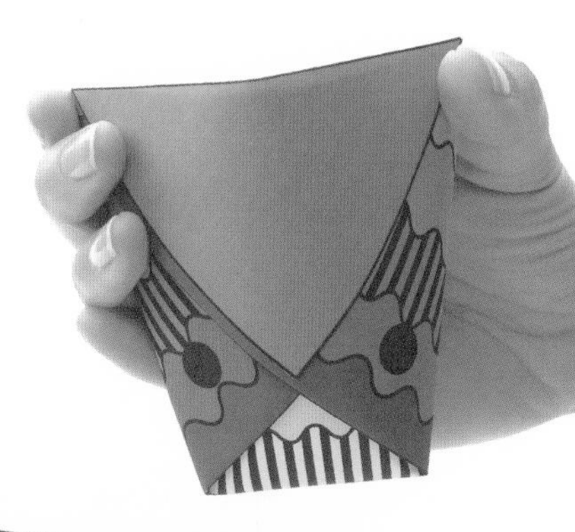

TEAR OFF COLORED SHEET ALONG THIS EDGE

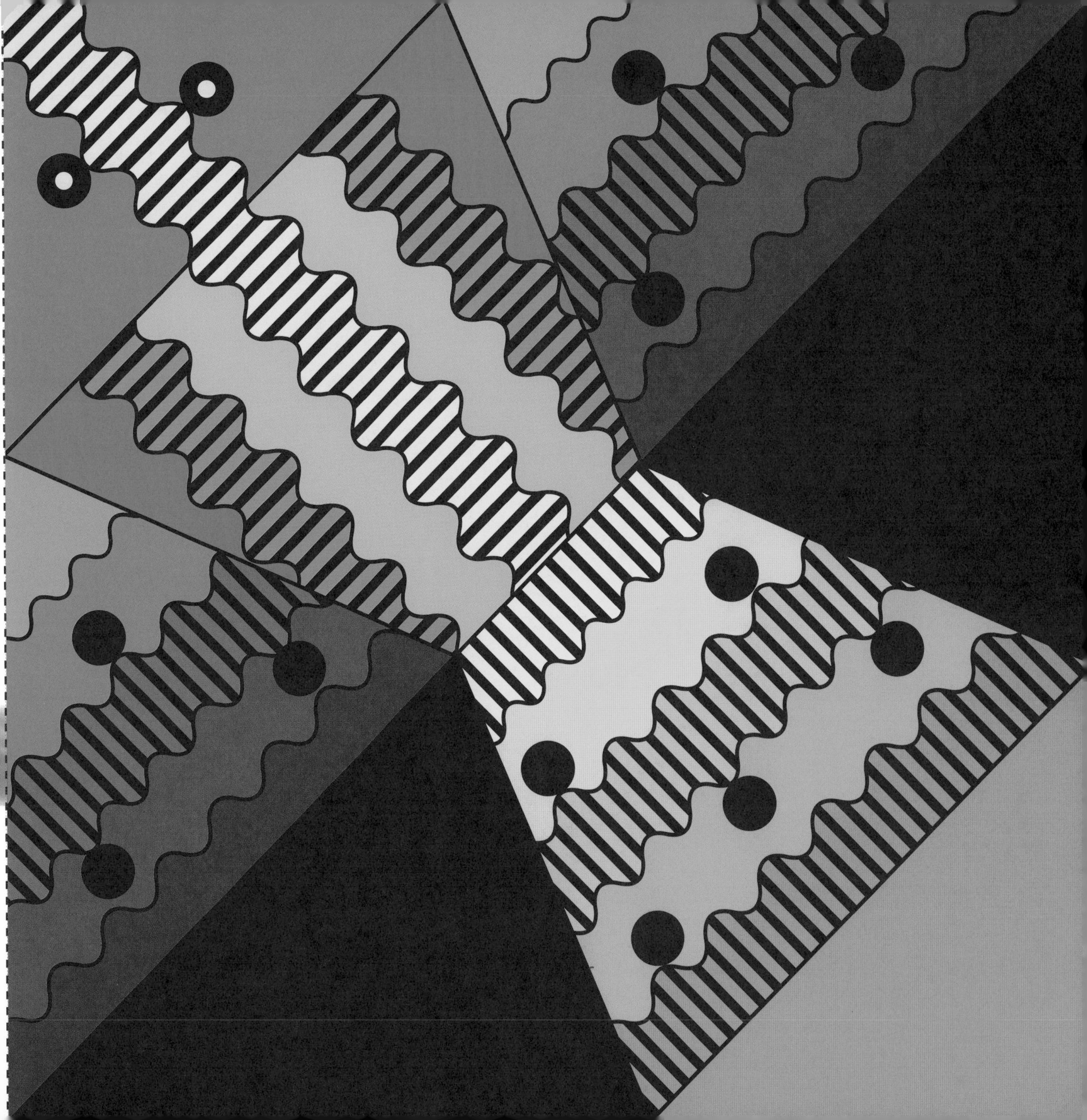

1

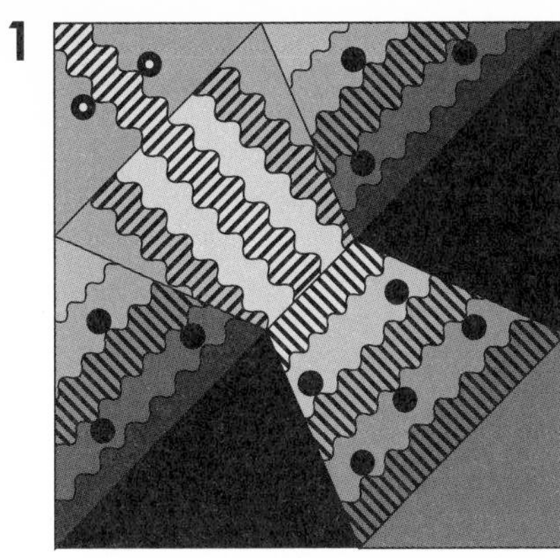

Turn over.

2

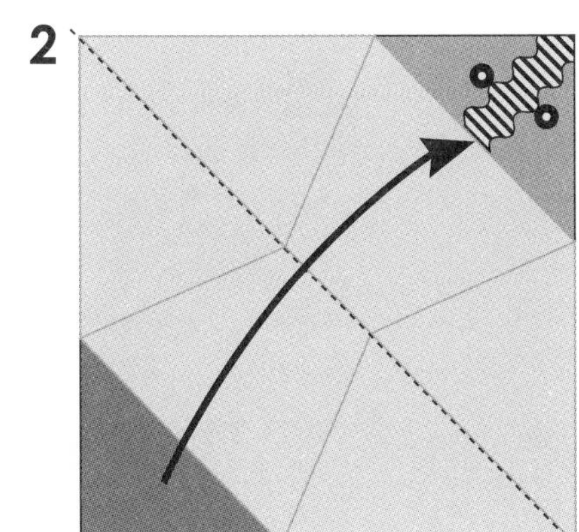

TEAR OFF COLORED SHEET ALONG THIS EDGE

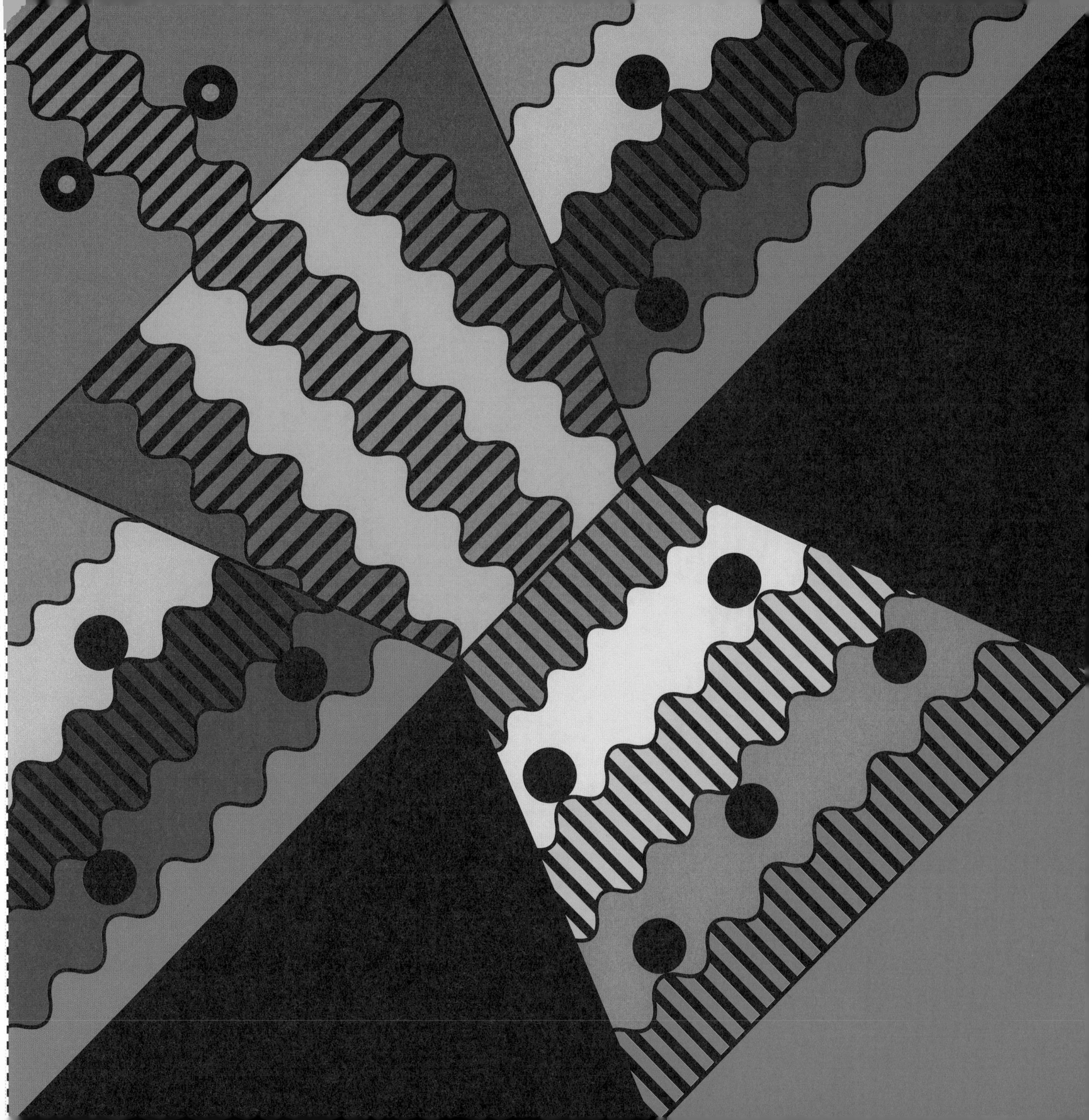

3

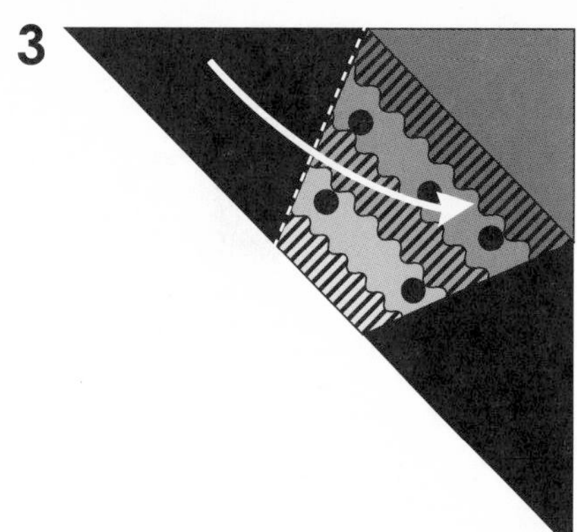

4

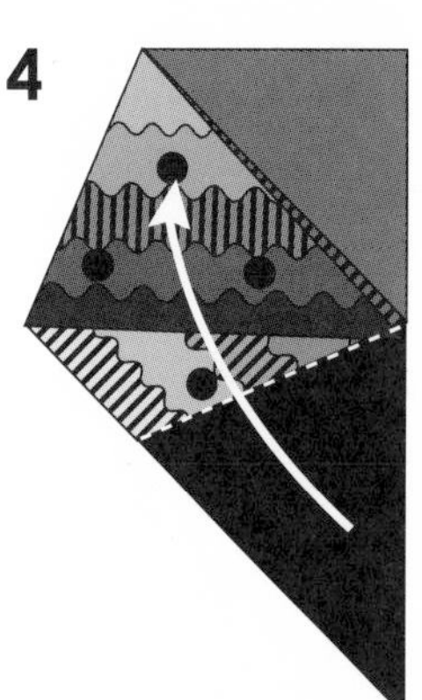

5

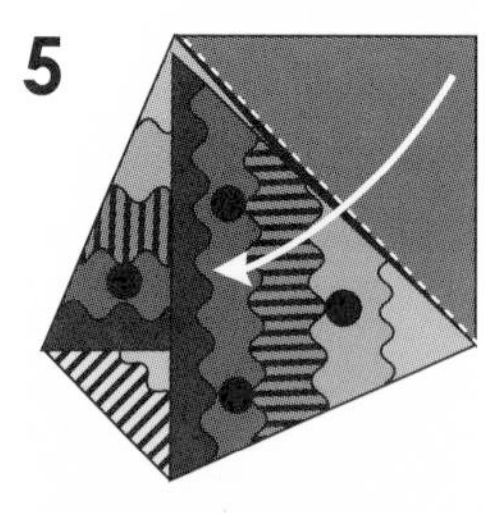

Valley fold just one side.

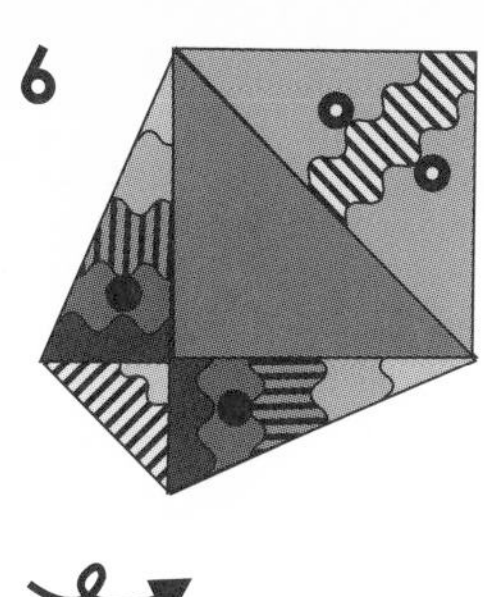

6

Turn over.

7

8

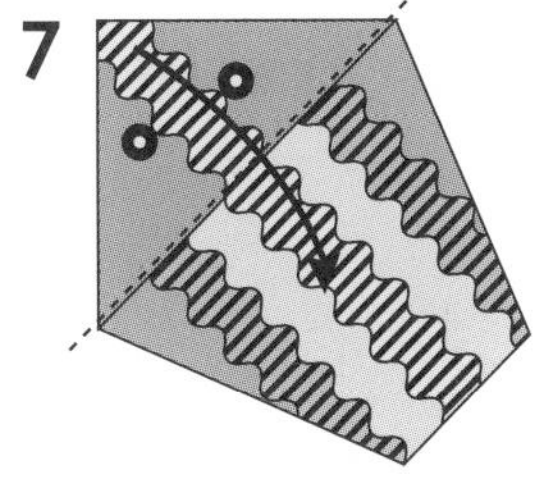

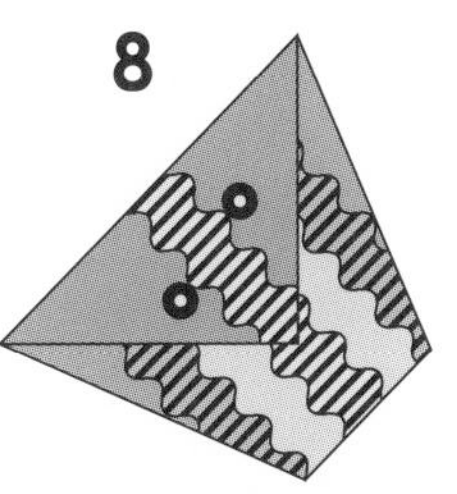

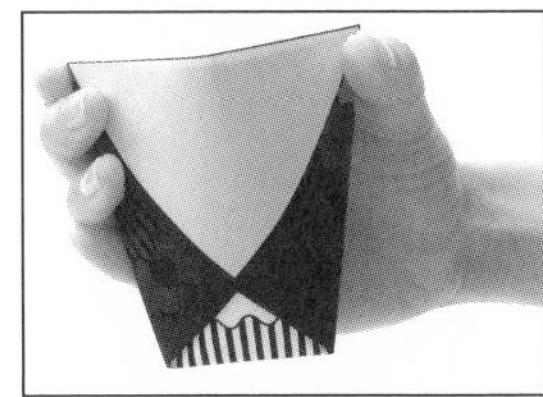

Push at the sides to spread open the interior and form a cup.

TEAR OFF COLORED SHEET ALONG THIS EDGE

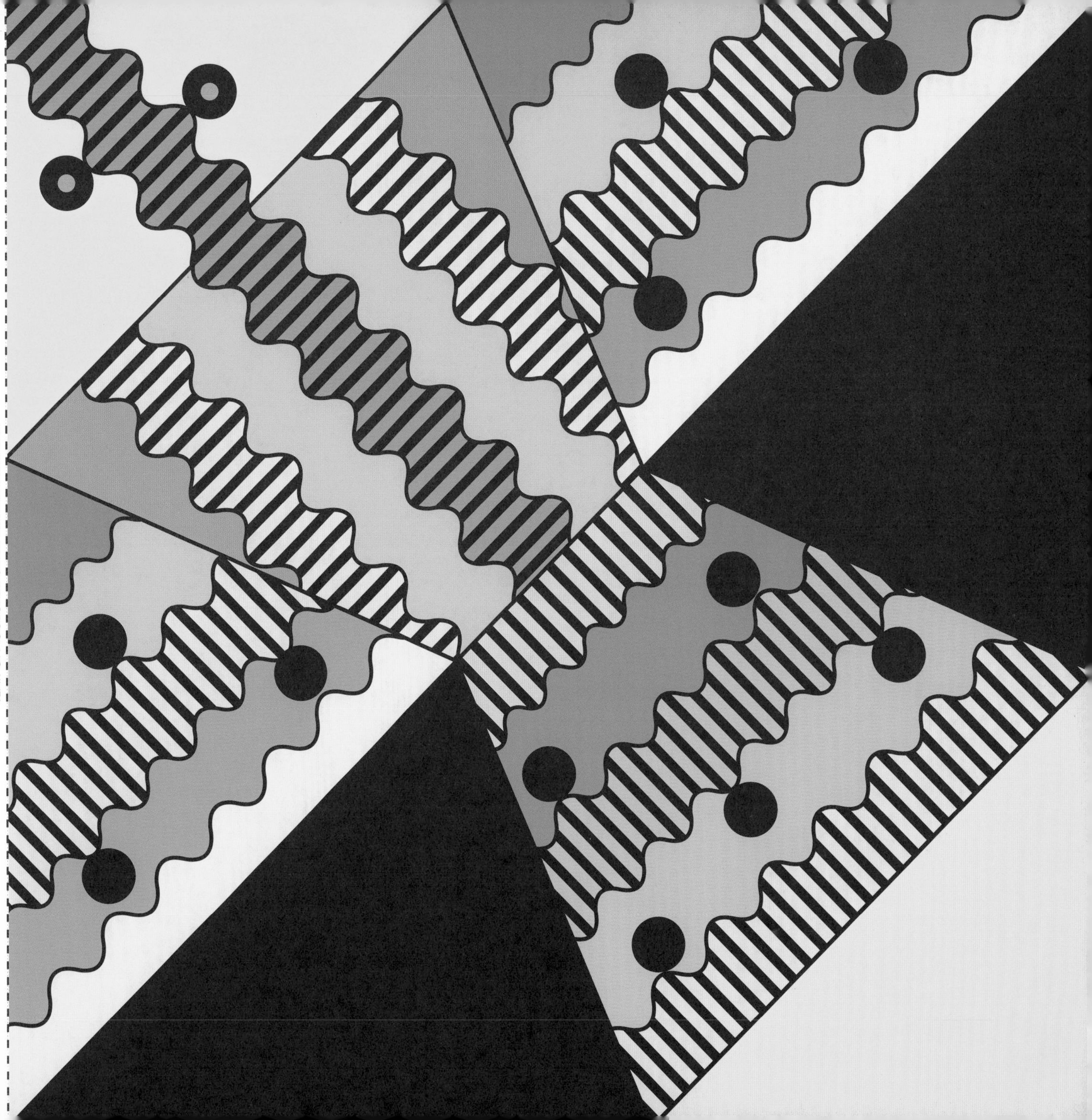

カオ

FACE
(Kao)

Smiling faces, surprised faces, sad faces. . . . All kinds of faces will pop up just by opening the paper one corner at a time. Great for playing Peek-a-Boo or entertaining the little ones with different faces. Which face resembles you?

TEAR OFF COLORED SHEET ALONG THIS EDGE

1

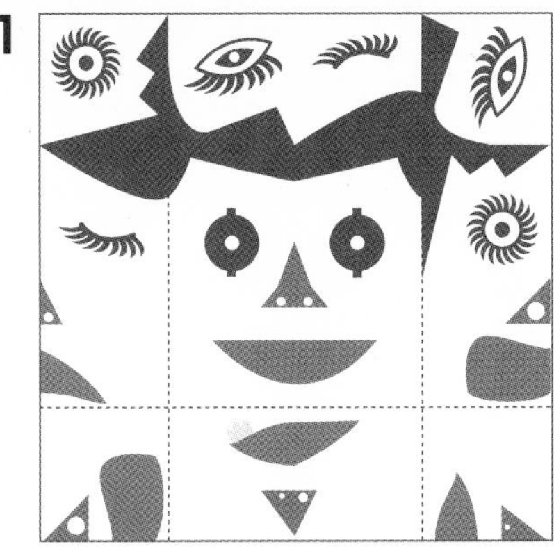

Turn over.

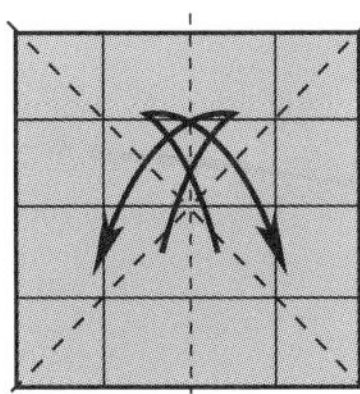

Fold and unfold in half, corner to corner, to make triangular creases.

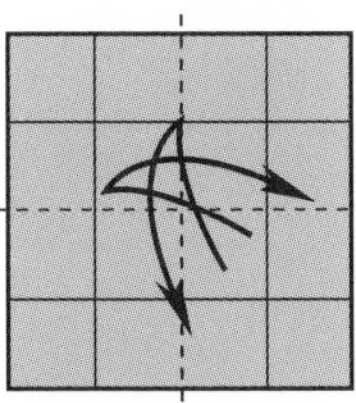

Fold and unfold in half again to make horizontal and vertical creases.

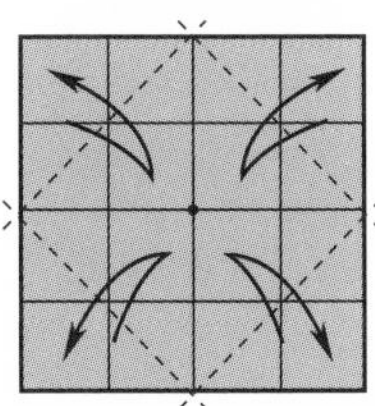

Now make shorter creases by folding and unfolding the corners to the center point.

TEAR OFF COLORED SHEET ALONG THIS EDGE

2

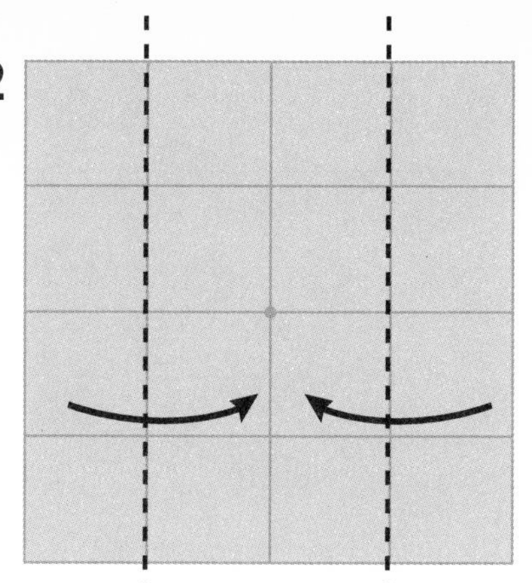

3

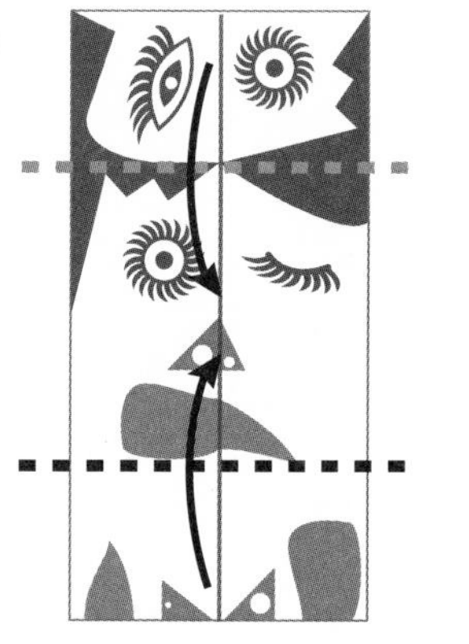

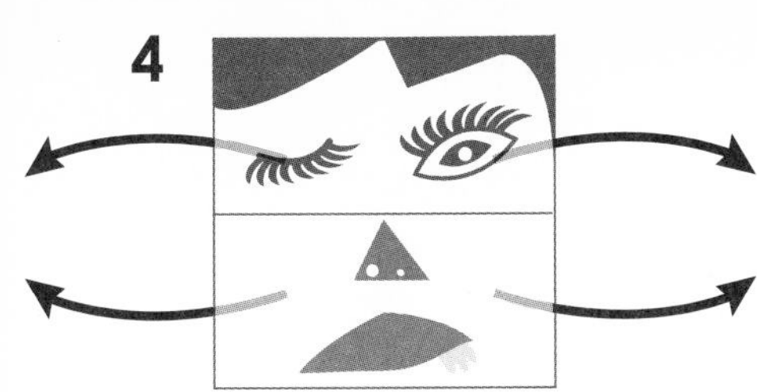

Pull out the corners from the inside.

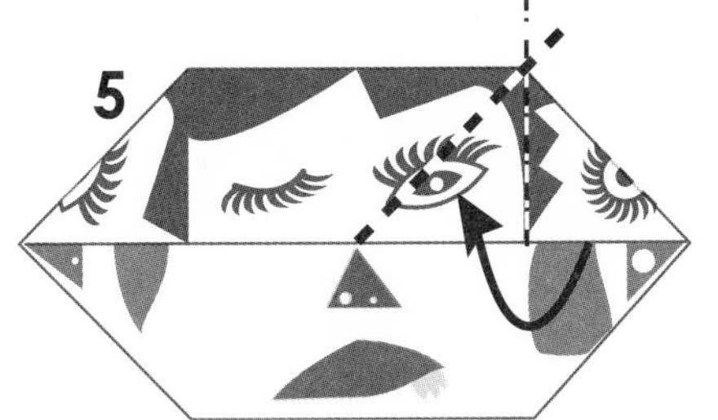

Push in as you fold up.

TEAR OFF COLORED SHEET ALONG THIS EDGE

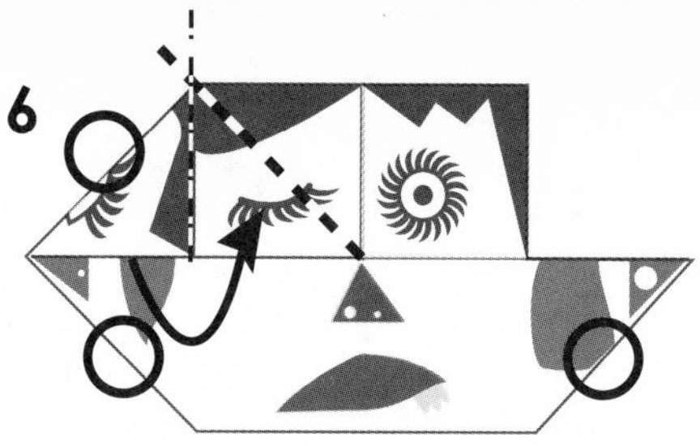

Repeat the action in step 5 on the remaining corners (circled edges).

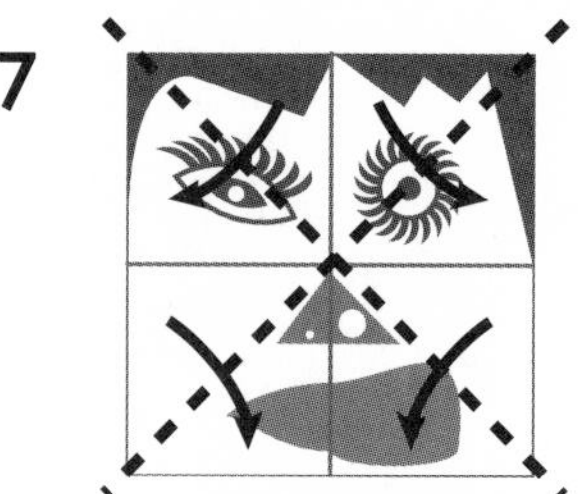

Now fold and unfold to make lots of different faces!

ユビニンギョウ

FINGER PUPPETS
(Yubiningyo)

From a single piece of paper come four dogs! Slip them on your fingertips and wiggle them around. You can also use them as covers for spoons and bottles. Kids will get a kick out of slipping them onto straws.

TEAR OFF COLORED SHEET ALONG THIS EDGE

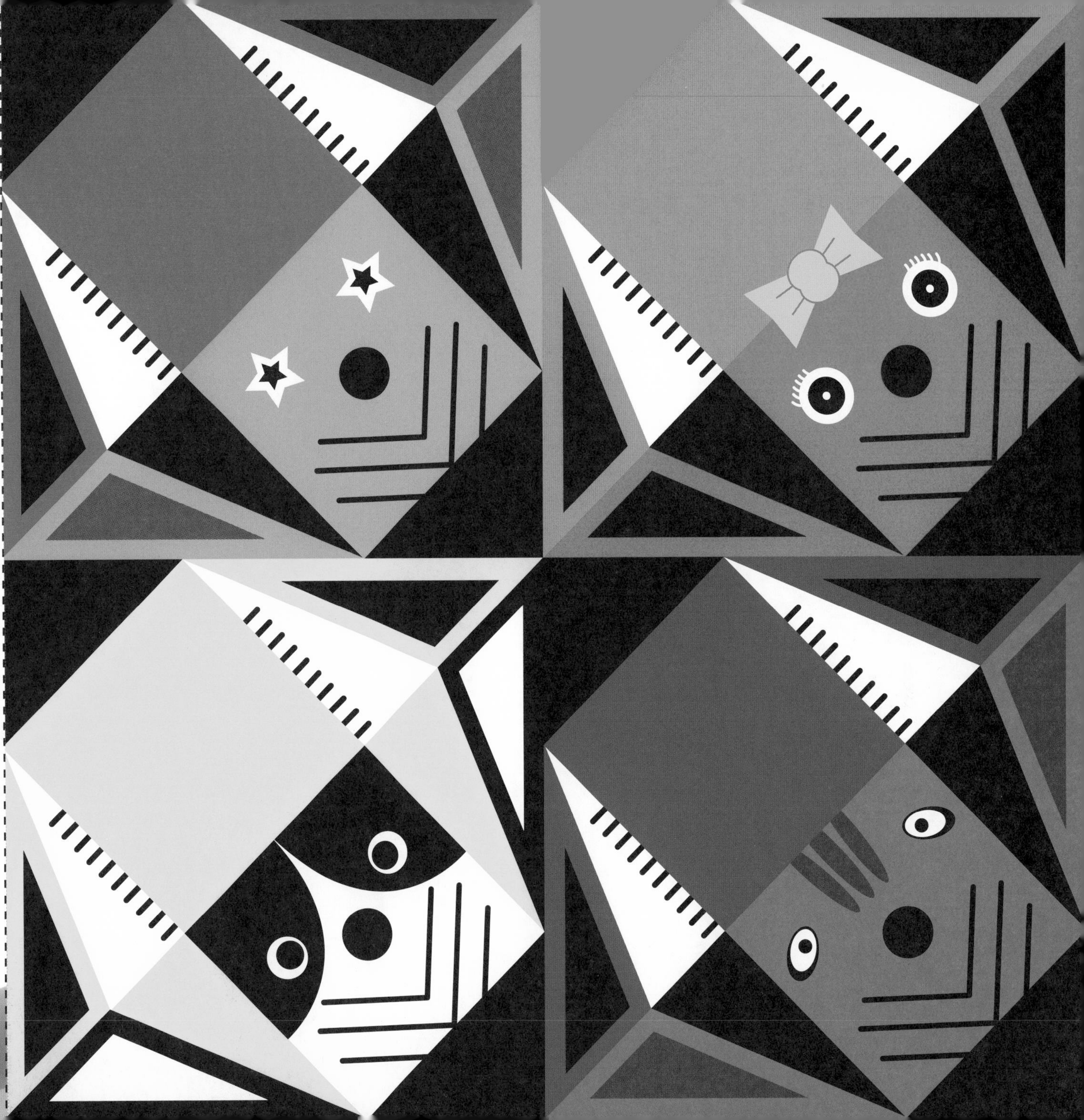

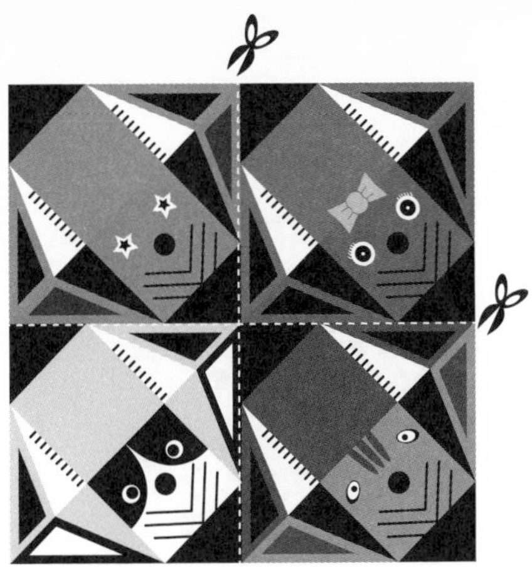

Use scissors to carefully cut the printed paper into four equal pieces.

For each of the four pieces, follow the steps below.

TEAR OFF COLORED SHEET ALONG THIS EDGE

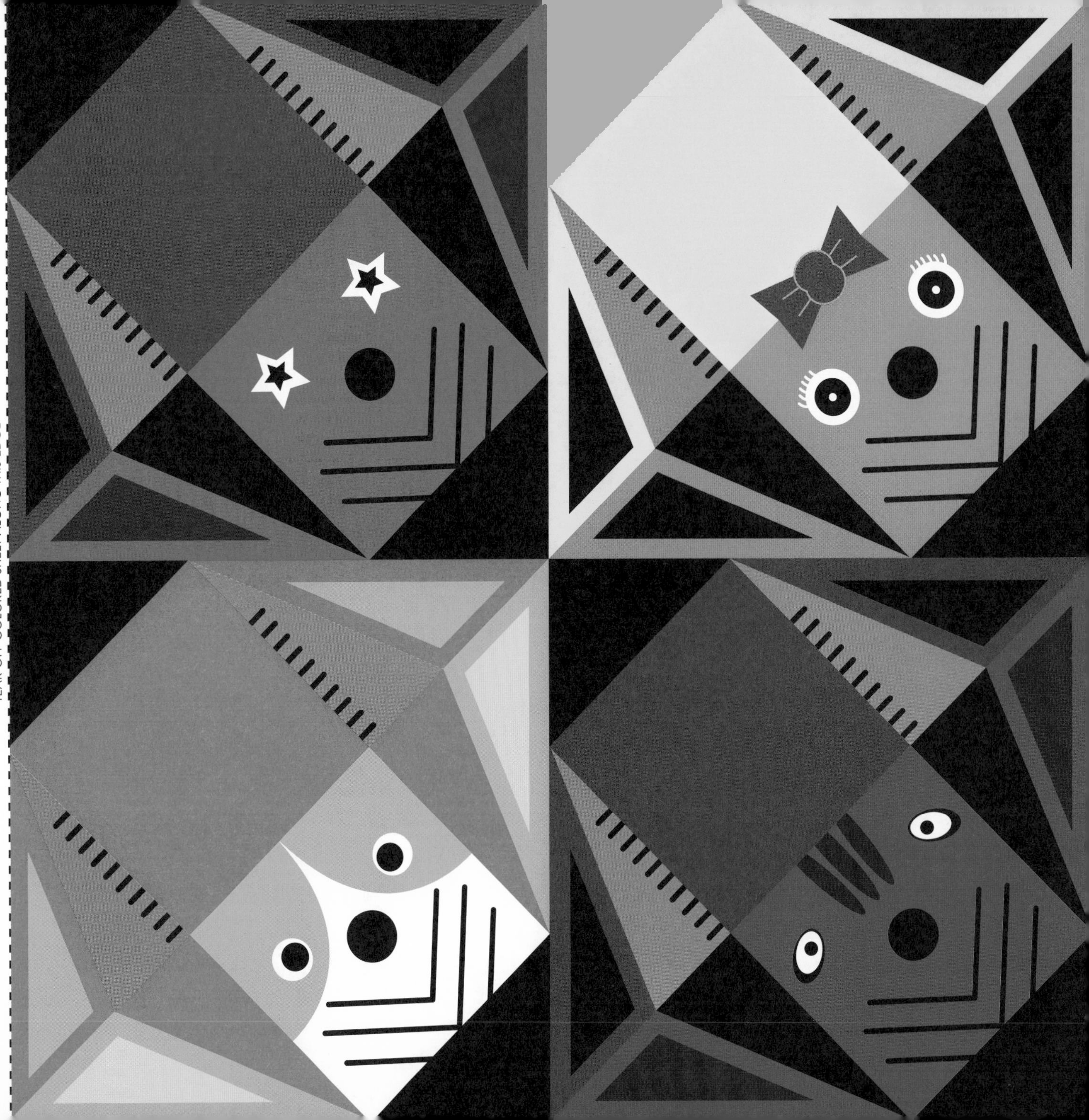

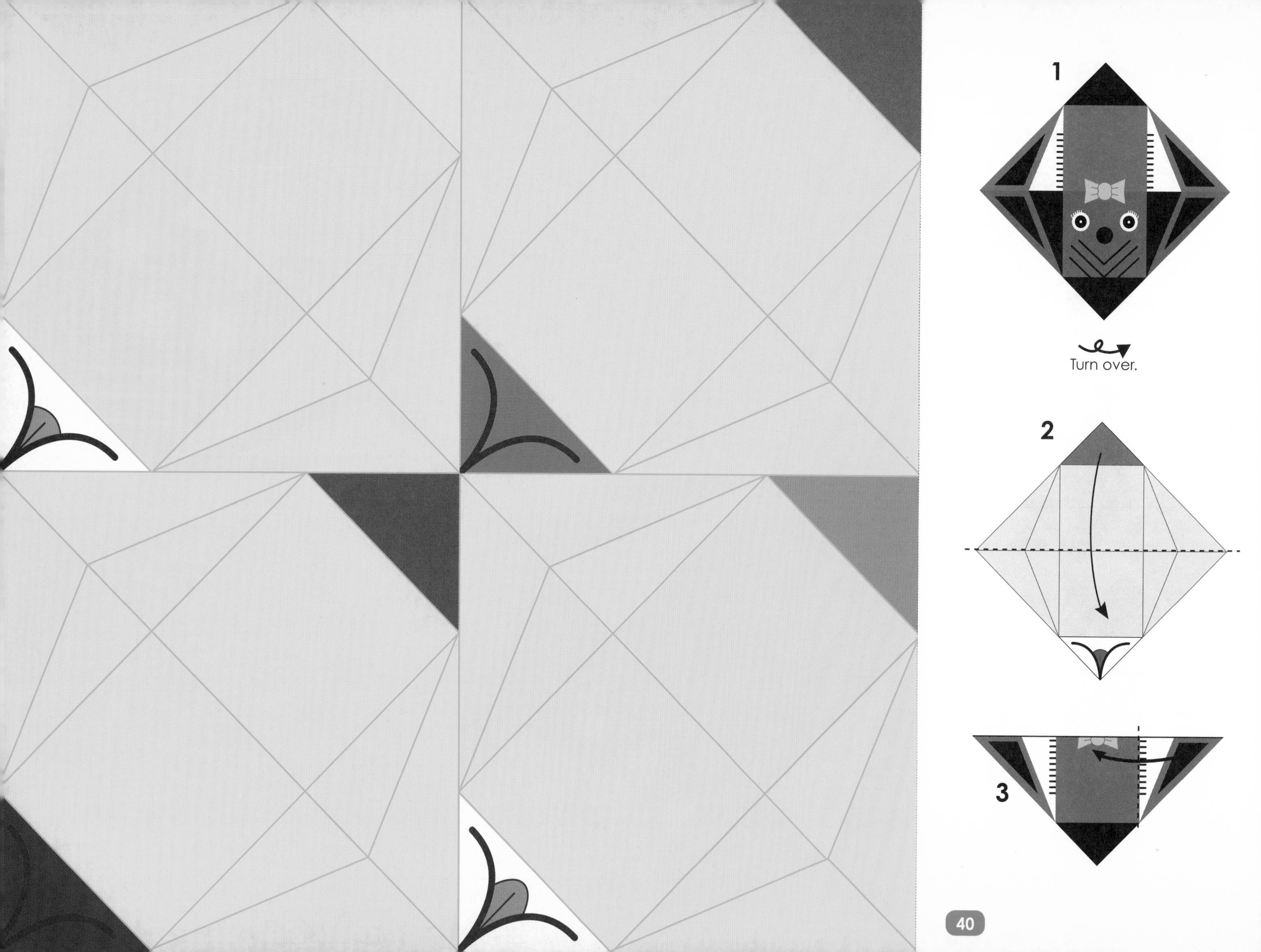

1
Turn over.
2
3

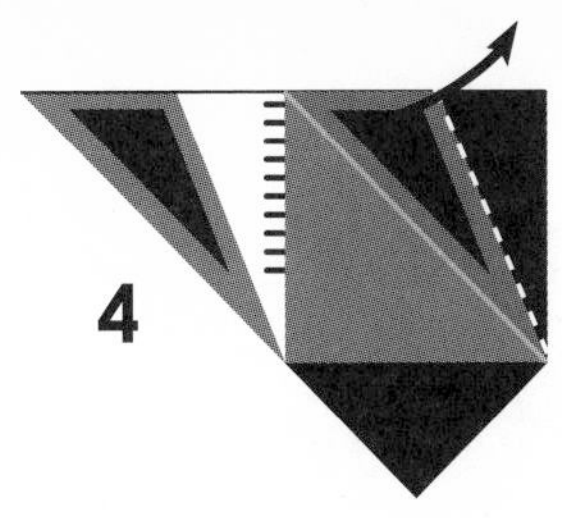

4

Valley fold to create the ear.

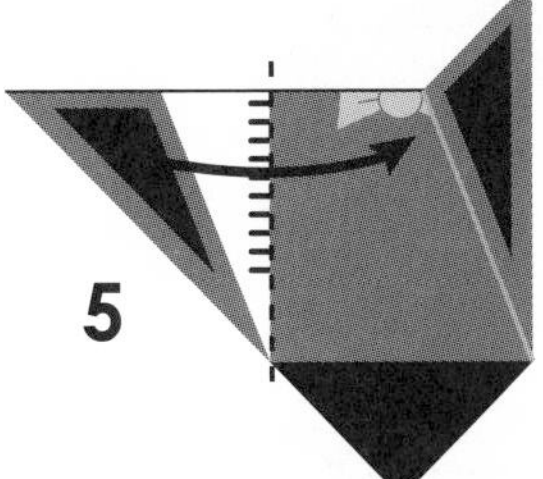

5

Repeat steps 3–4 on the opposite side.

6

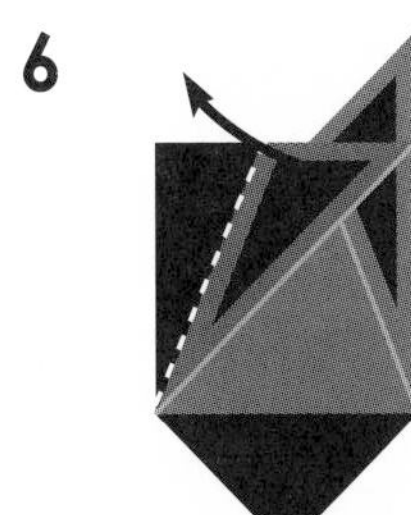

7

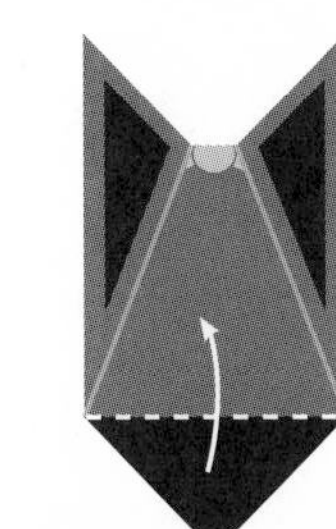

Valley fold only the top sheet upward.

TEAR OFF COLORED SHEET ALONG THIS EDGE

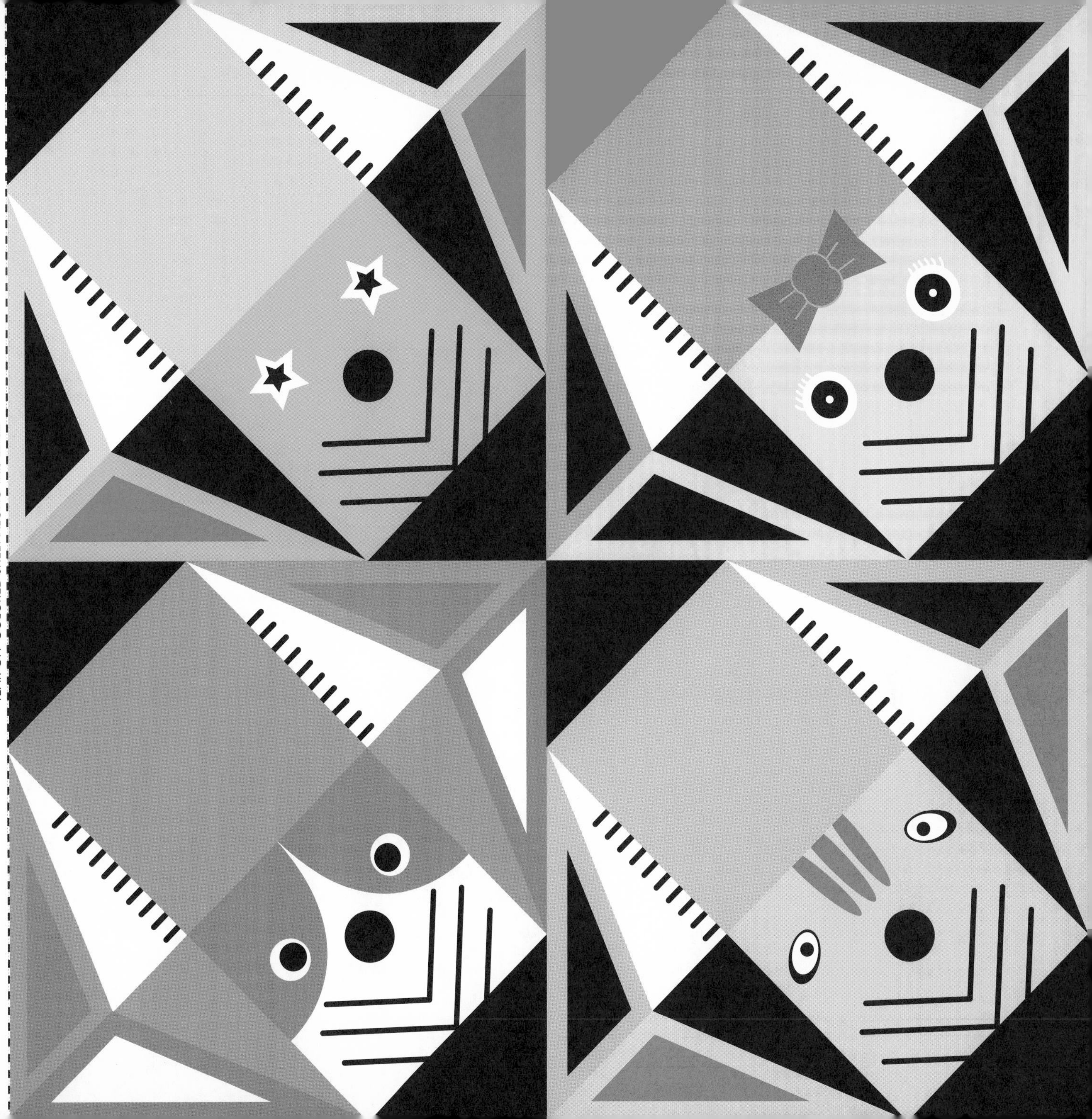

8

Turn over.

9

10

Now do the same with the other 3 pieces. Arrange the puppets on your fingertips and put on a show!

パタパタツル

FLAPPING CRANE
(Patapata-tsuru)

This beautiful crane is also a graceful flier. While holding the neck, pull the tail to flap the crane's wings. Your virtual flying crane is complete! Now use it to put on a puppet show.

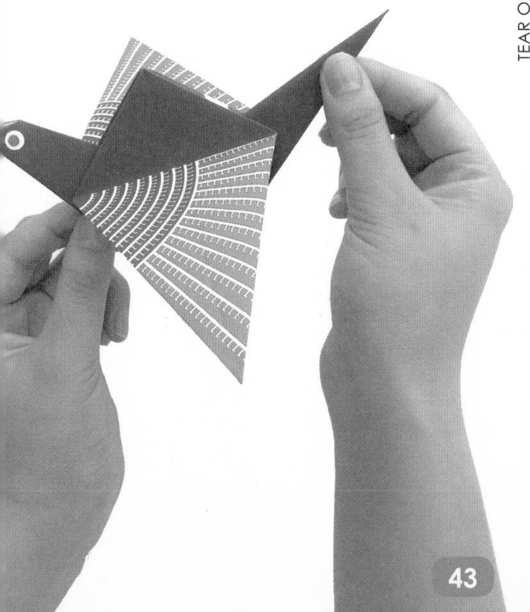

TEAR OFF COLORED SHEET ALONG THIS EDGE

1

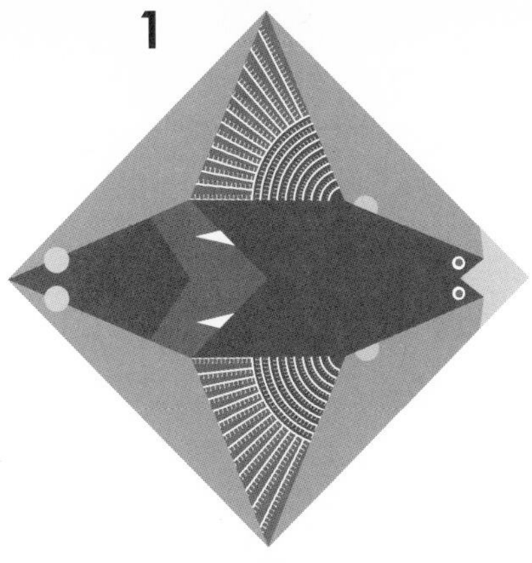

Turn over.

2

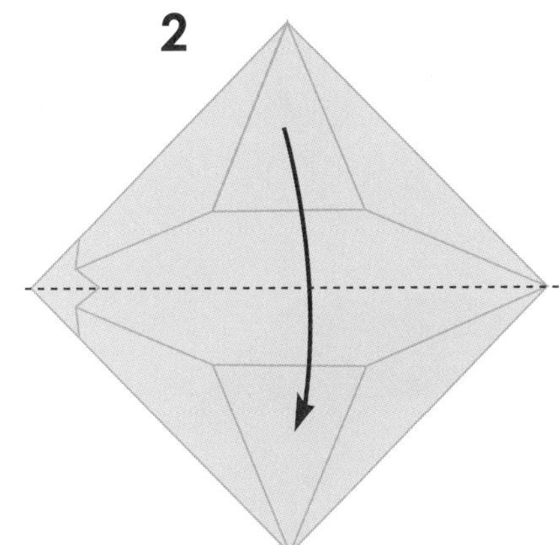

3

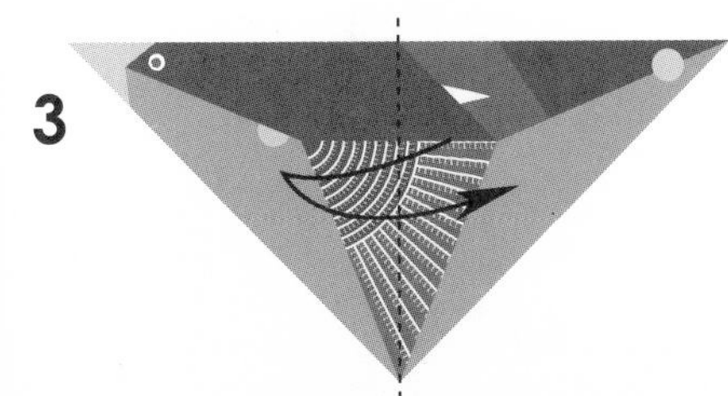

Make a crease as shown.

TEAR OFF COLORED SHEET ALONG THIS EDGE

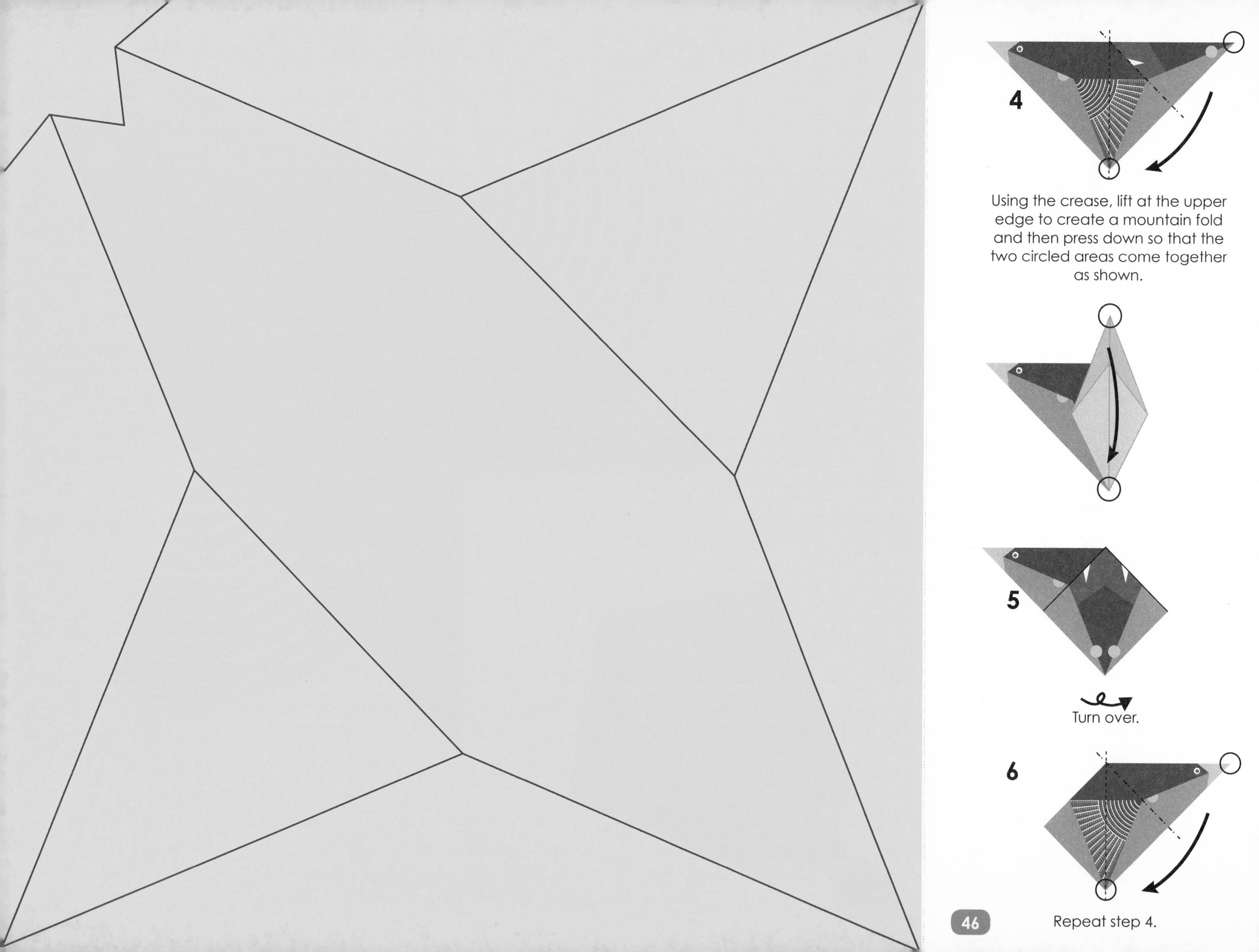
4
Using the crease, lift at the upper edge to create a mountain fold and then press down so that the two circled areas come together as shown.
5
Turn over.
6
Repeat step 4.

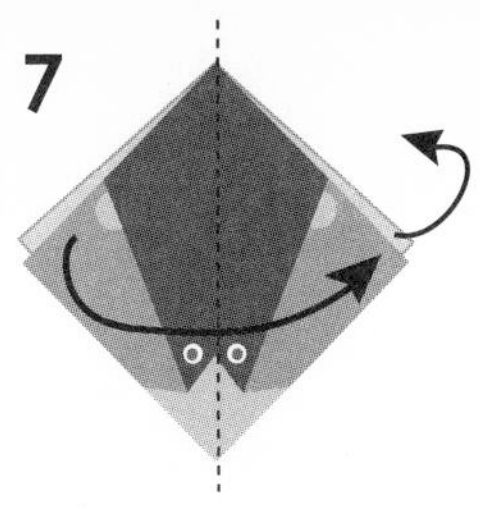

7

Fold open a single layer to reveal the design on the other side.

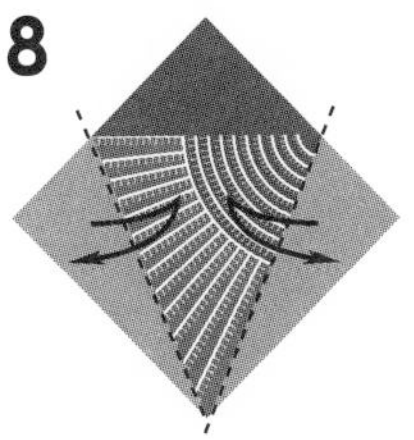

8

Create creases as shown.

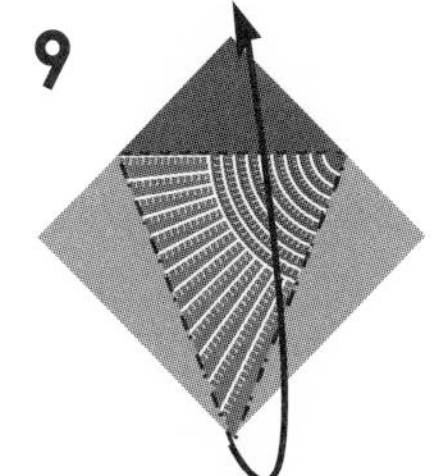

9

Using the creases, pull the bottom corner up as you press down.

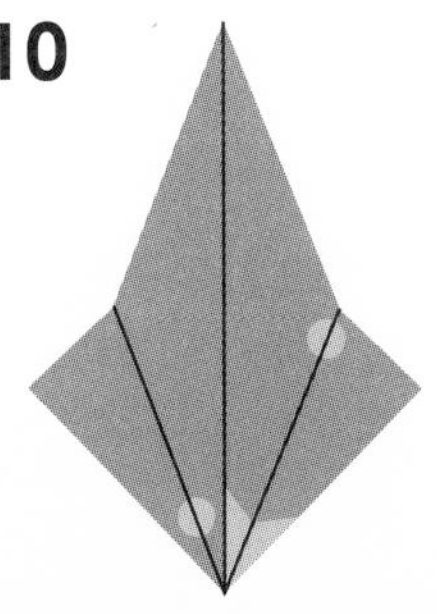

10

On the opposite side, repeat steps 8–10.

TEAR OFF COLORED SHEET ALONG THIS EDGE

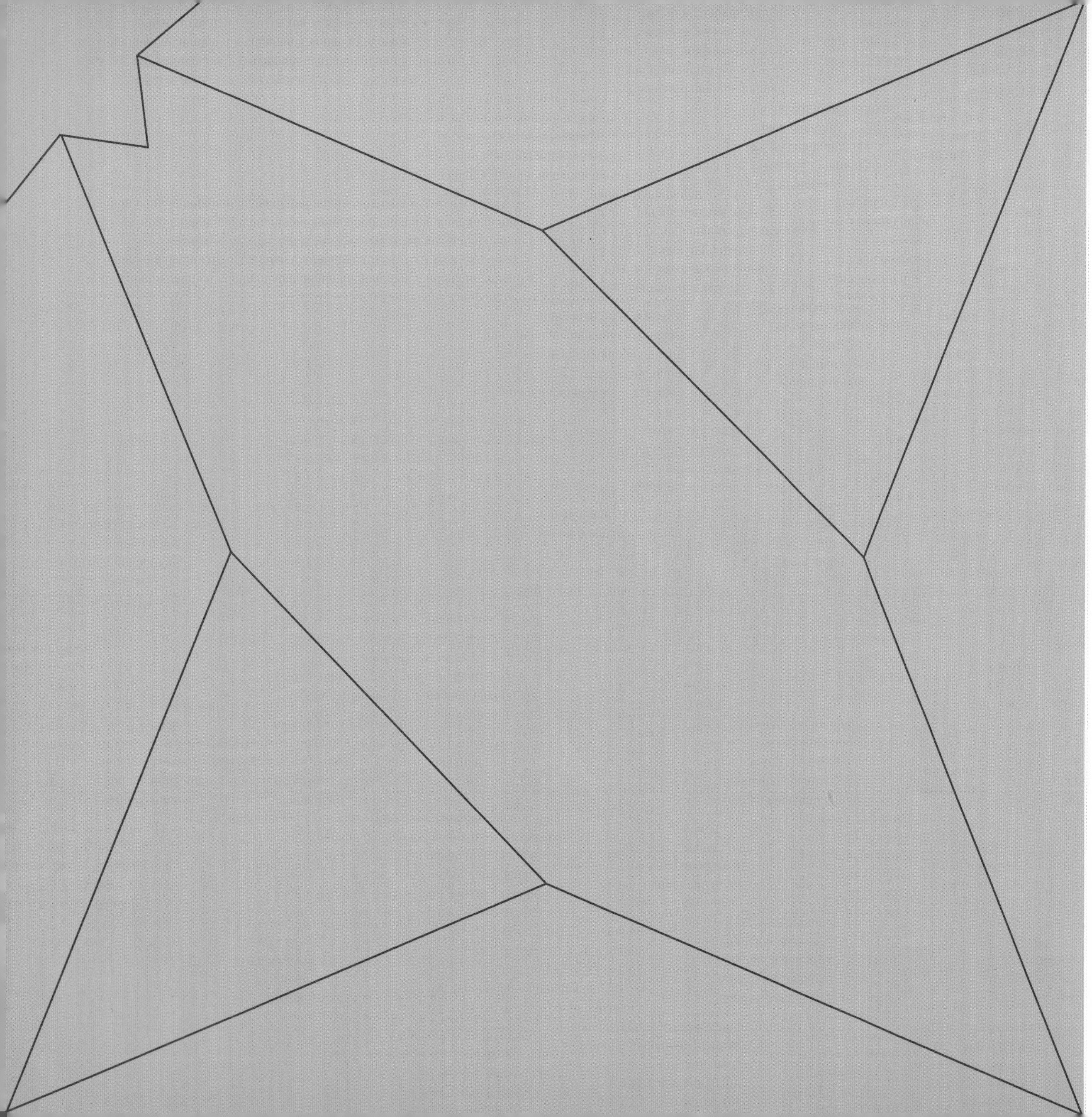

11

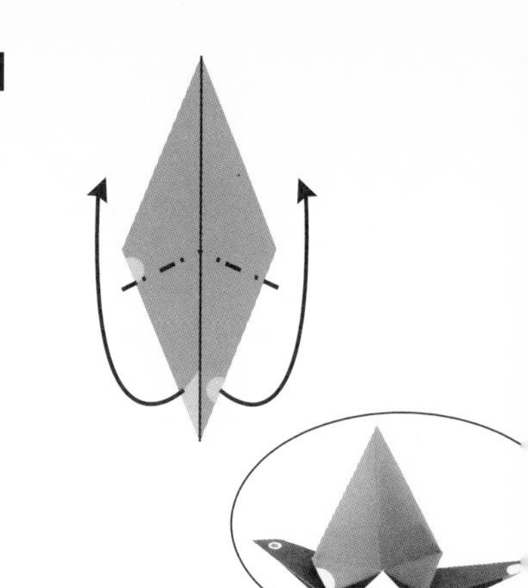

Use inside reverse folds to create the head and tail.

12

Use a small inside reverse fold to create the beak.

13

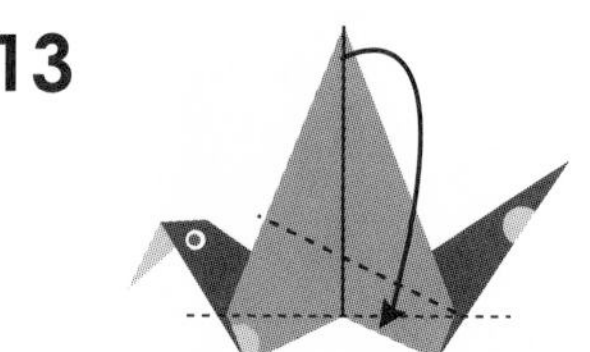

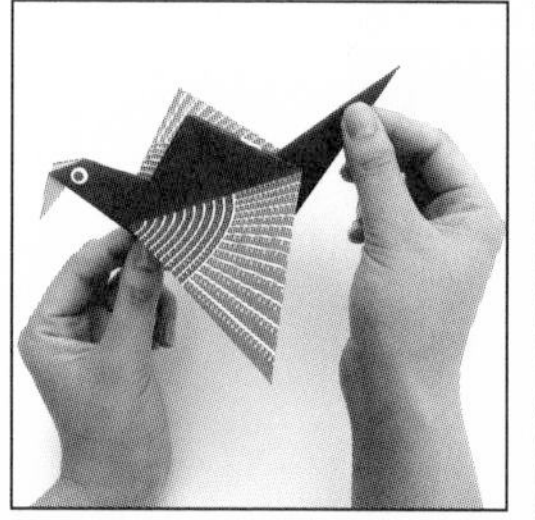

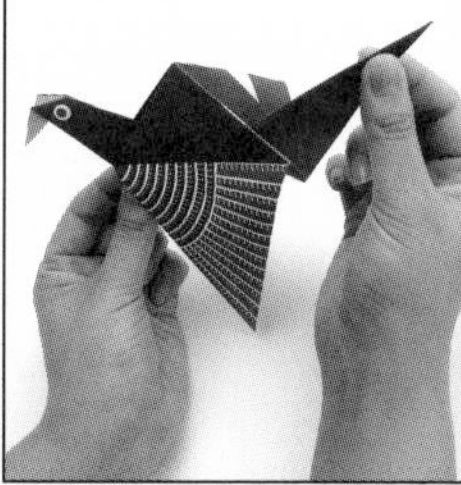

Holding the crane as shown, pull its tail to make its wings flap.

マルバツアソビ

FORTUNE TELLER
(Marubatsu-asobi)

"O" (right) and "X" (wrong) appear as you open and close your fingers. Have your friend pick a number, then open and close that same number of times to get your answer. Now ask it a question and keep playing to predict your future. Is your horoscope for today "O" or "X"?

TEAR OFF COLORED SHEET ALONG THIS EDGE

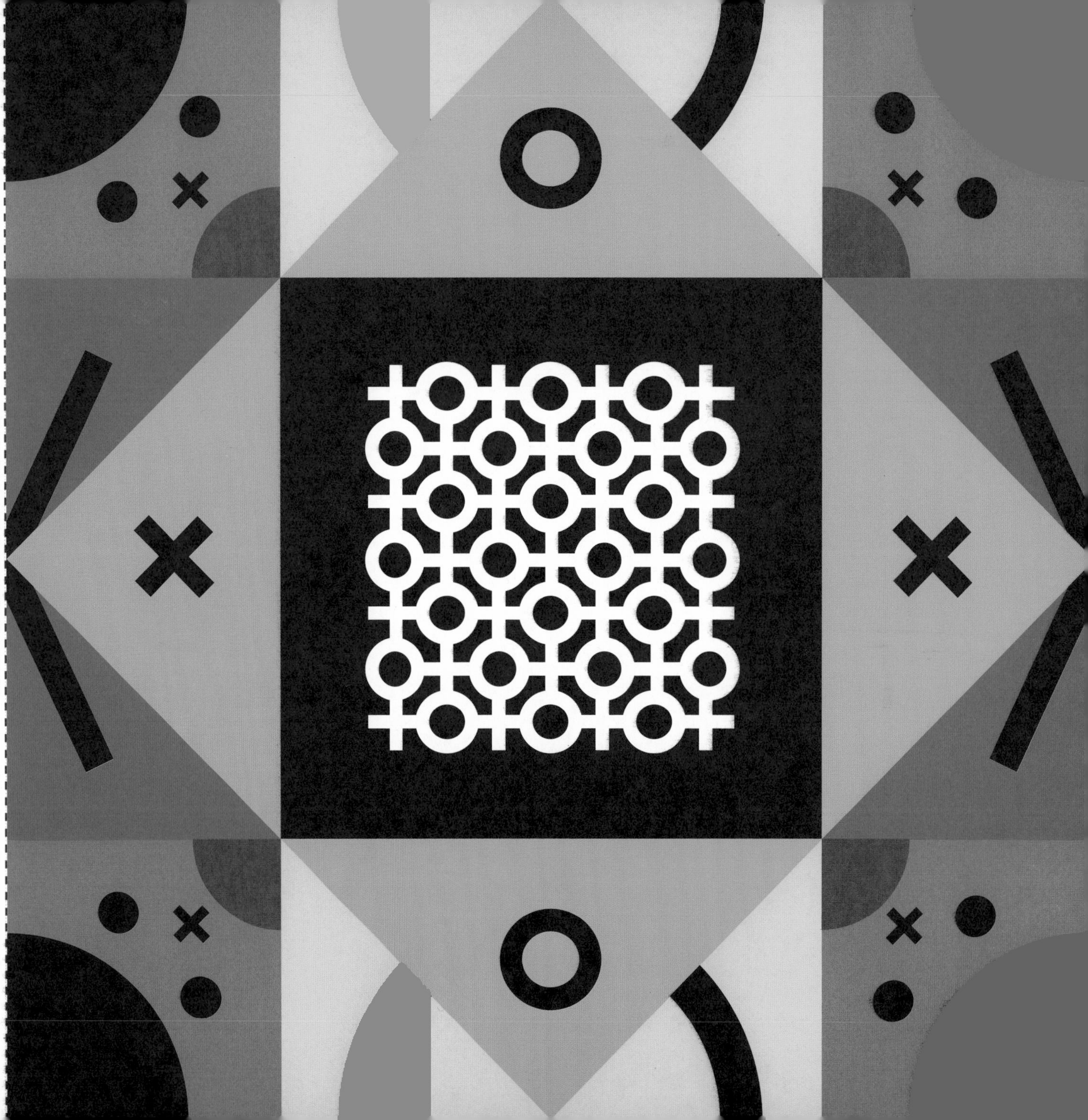

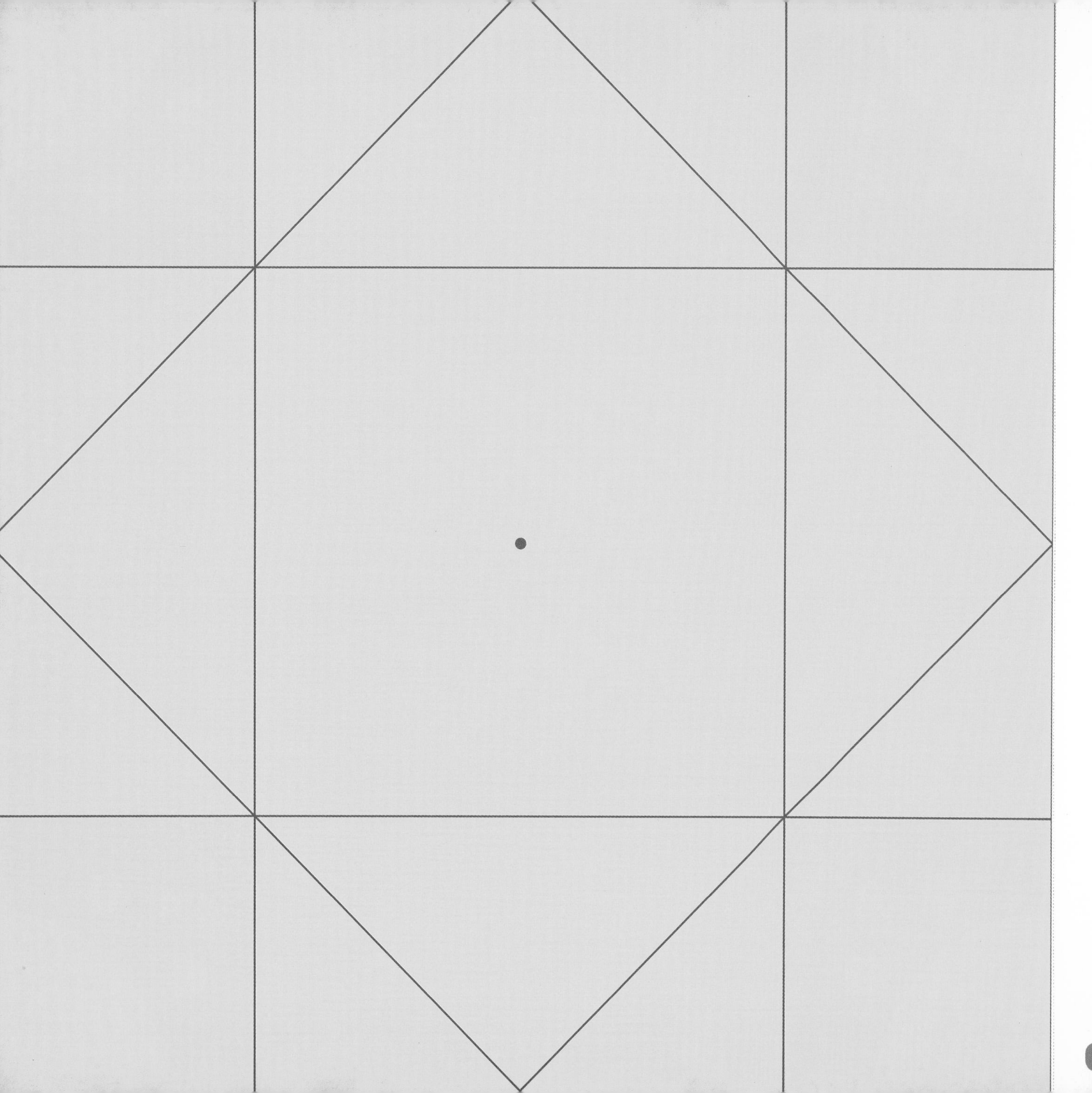

1

Turn over.

2

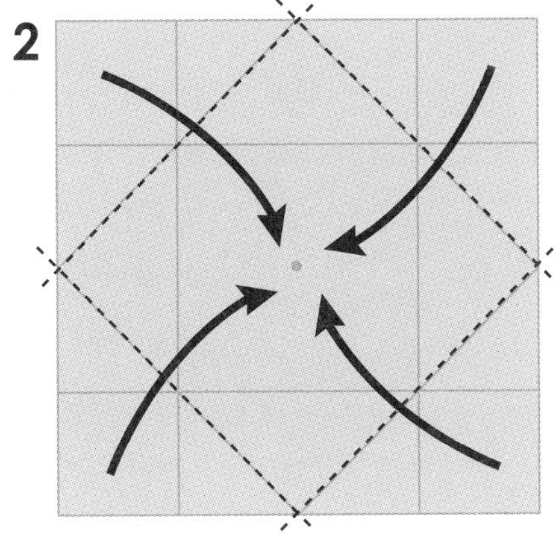

Valley fold the four corners to meet at the center.

TEAR OFF COLORED SHEET ALONG THIS EDGE

3

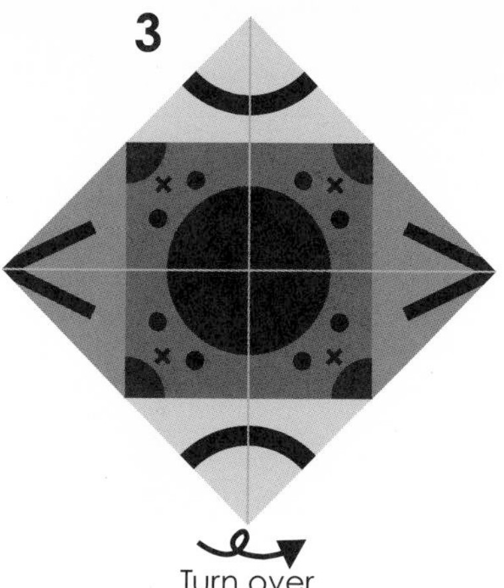

Turn over.

4

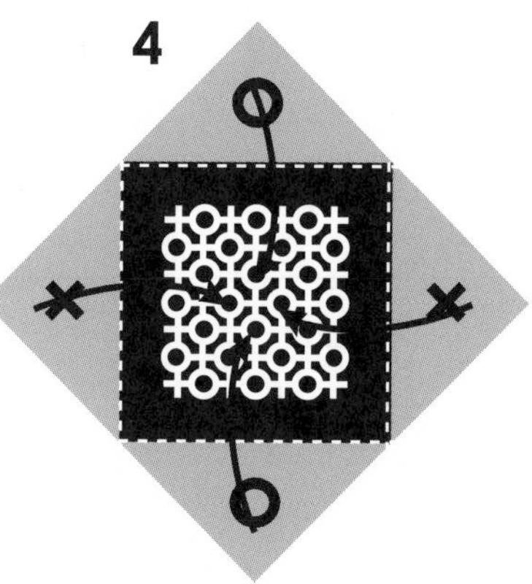

Valley fold the four corners to meet at the center.

5

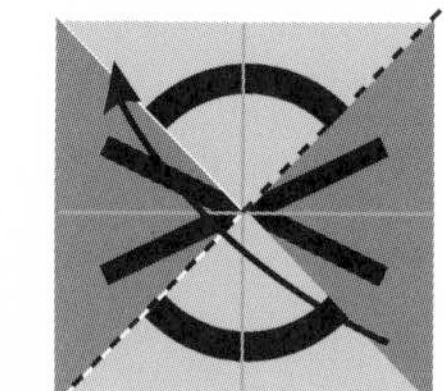

6

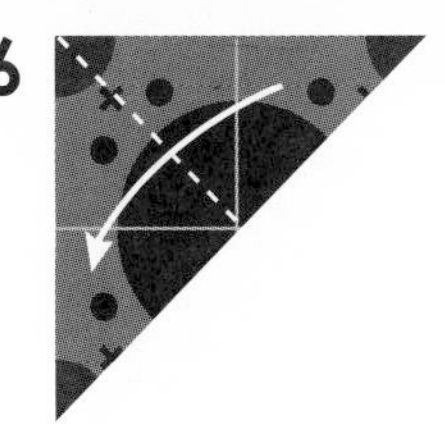

7

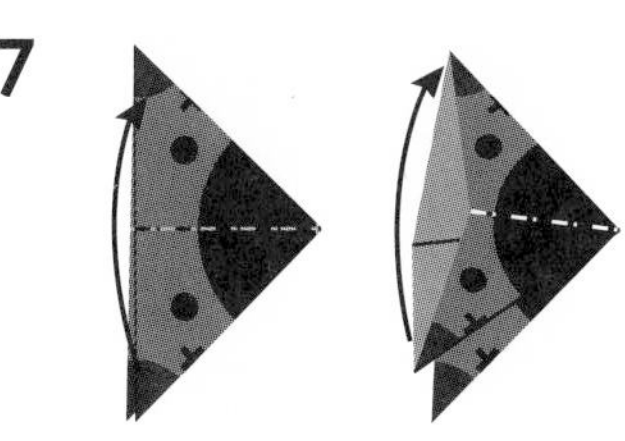

Pull open the inside as you press down.

8

Turn over.

9

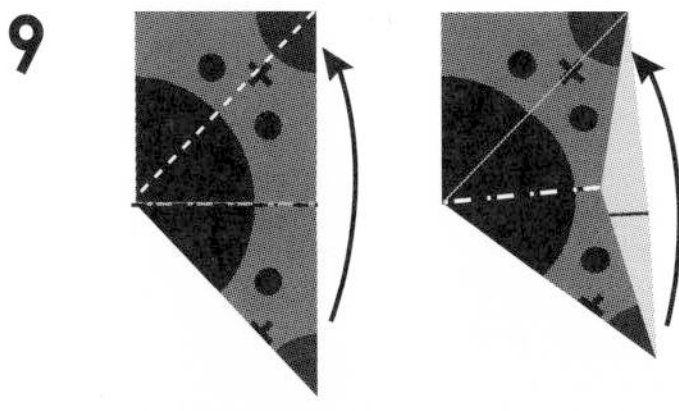

Pull open the inside as you press down.

TEAR OFF COLORED SHEET ALONG THIS EDGE

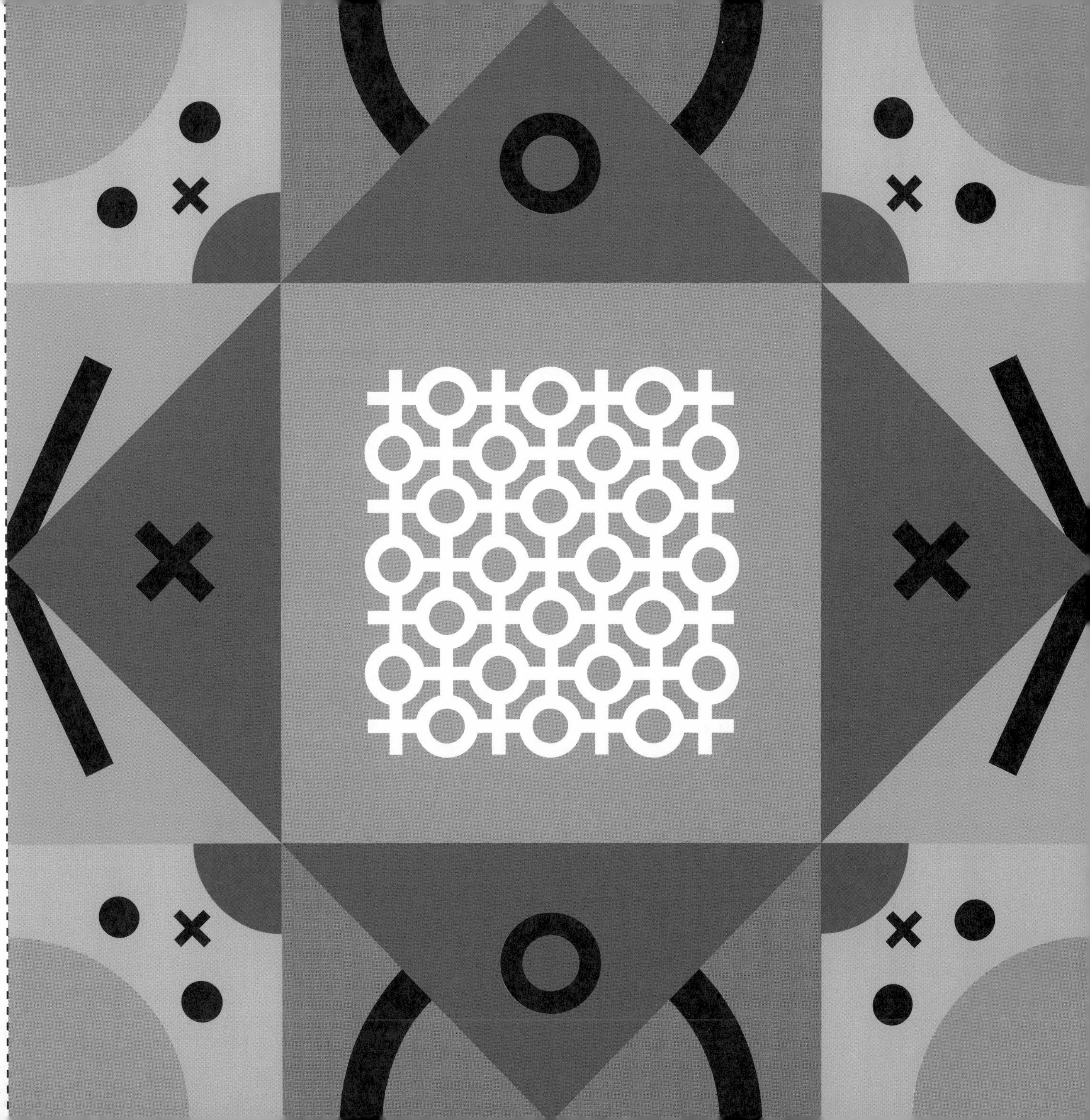

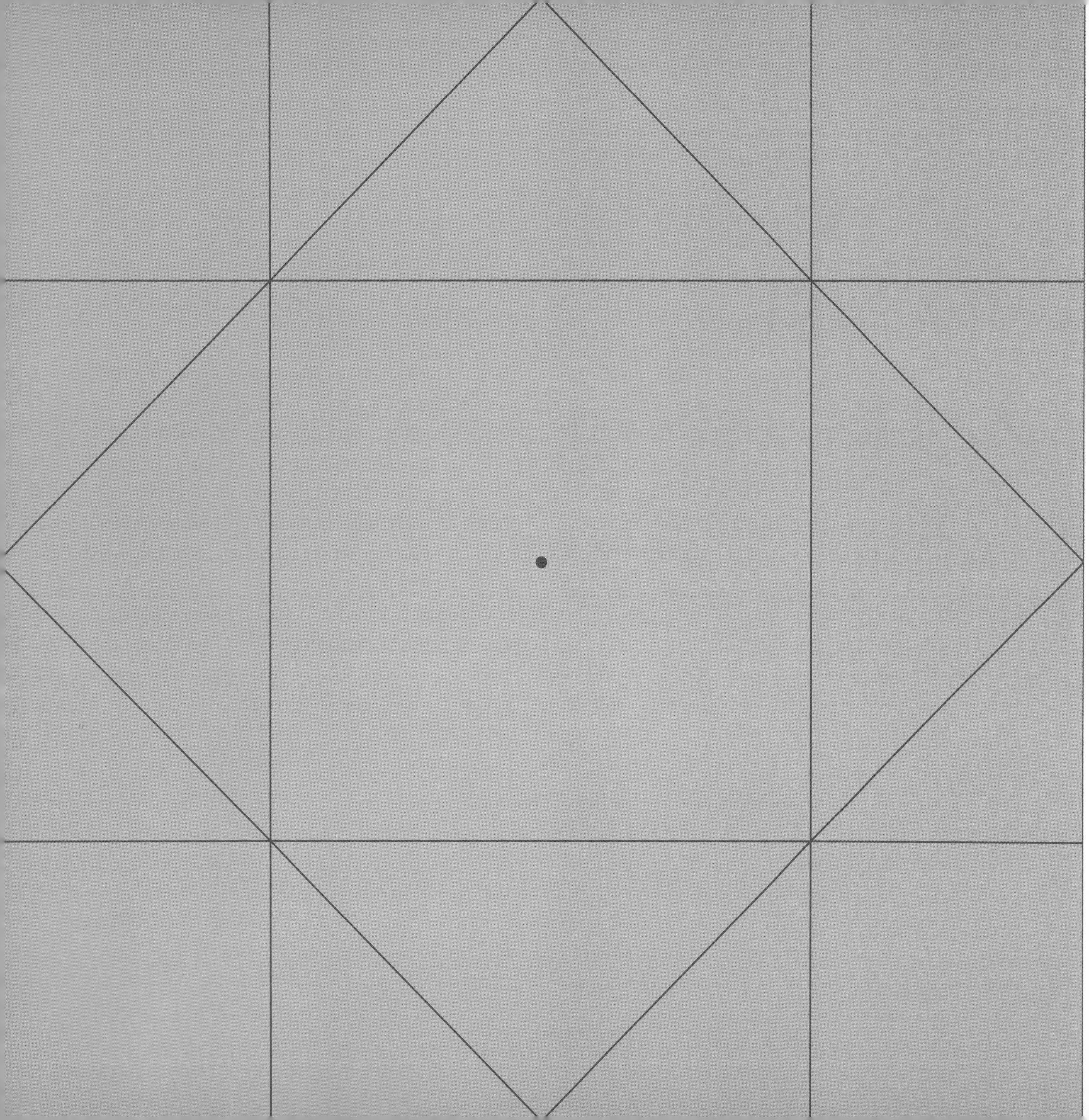

10

Turn counter-clockwise.

11

Push open from the inside to puff up.

Insert thumbs and index fingers as shown. Alternately pinch and spread open to reveal yes ("O") and no ("X") answers to your questions!

メガネ

GLASSES
(Megane)

Put them on your knuckle and play! They'll fit nicely on your face, too. What color glasses should we wear today? Try them all and put on a fashion show. You can't see in front of you, so be careful!

TEAR OFF COLORED SHEET ALONG THIS EDGE

1

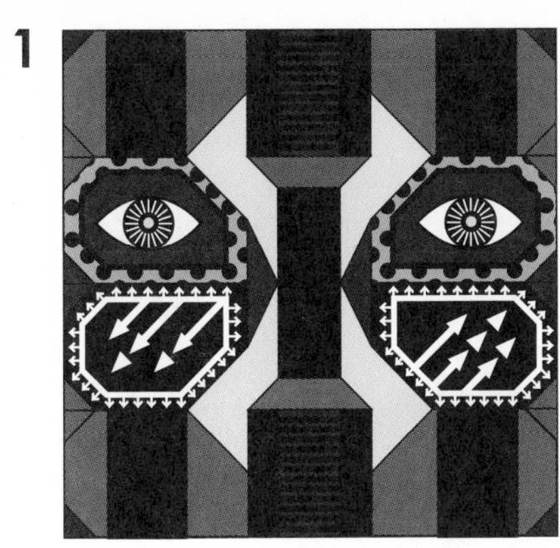

Turn over.

2

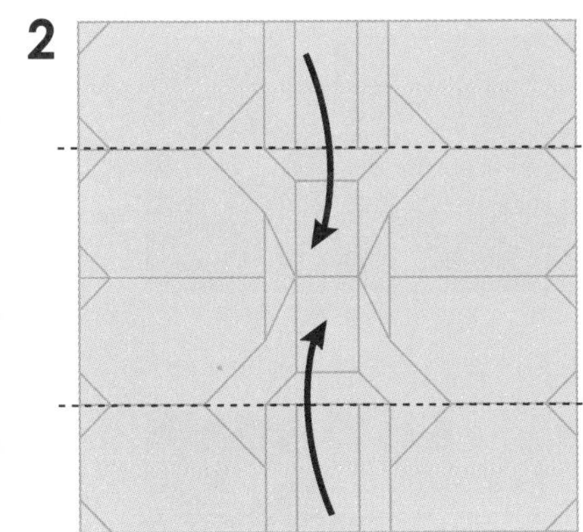

TEAR OFF COLORED SHEET ALONG THIS EDGE

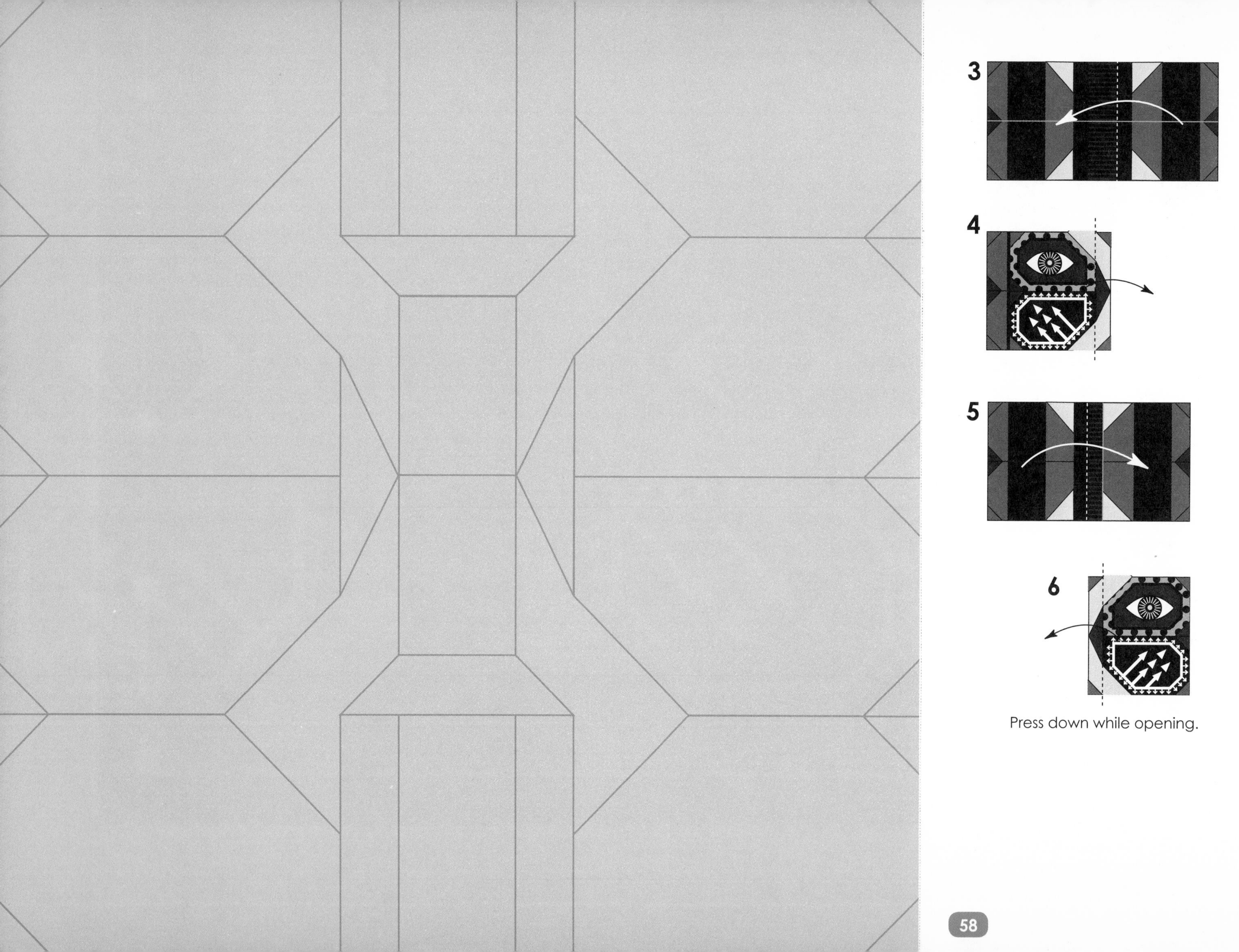

3

4

5

6

Press down while opening.

7

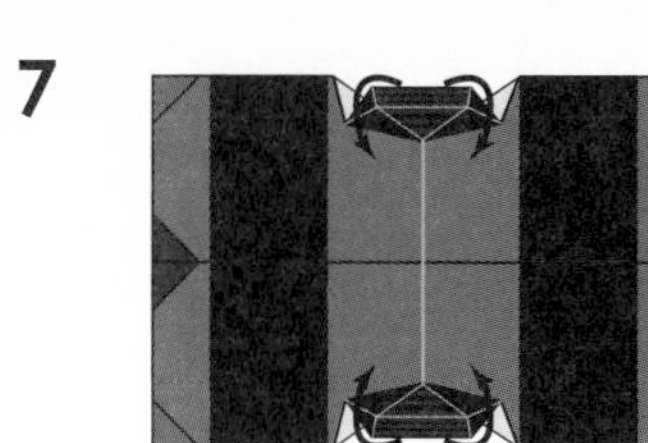

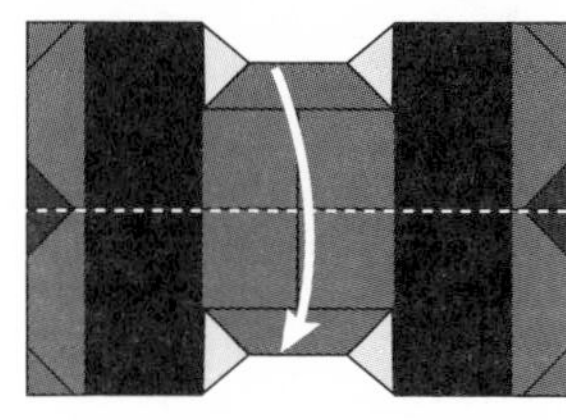

Make mountain folds at the corners as shown.

10

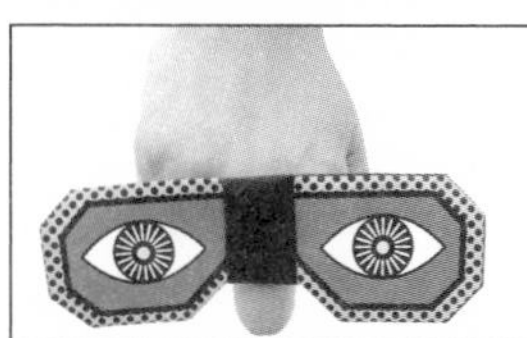

Use inside reverse folds to hide the exposed corners on the inside.

TEAR OFF COLORED SHEET ALONG THIS EDGE

イエ

HOUSE
(Ie)

Change the folds a little bit and you can create all kinds of houses. Try making your favorite house. Now line up a series of different houses and create your own neighborhood.

TEAR OFF COLORED SHEET ALONG THIS EDGE

1

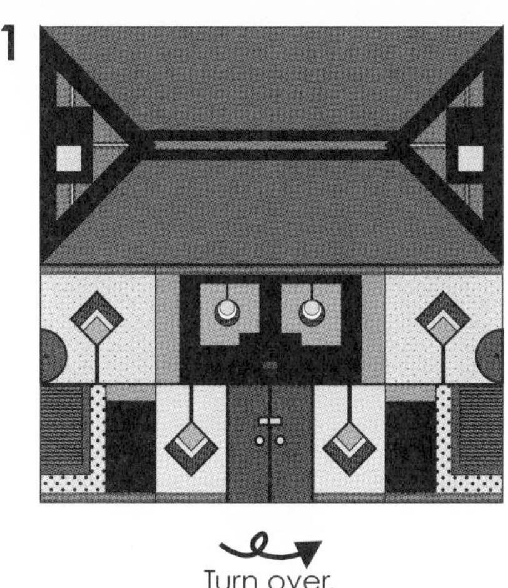

Turn over.

2

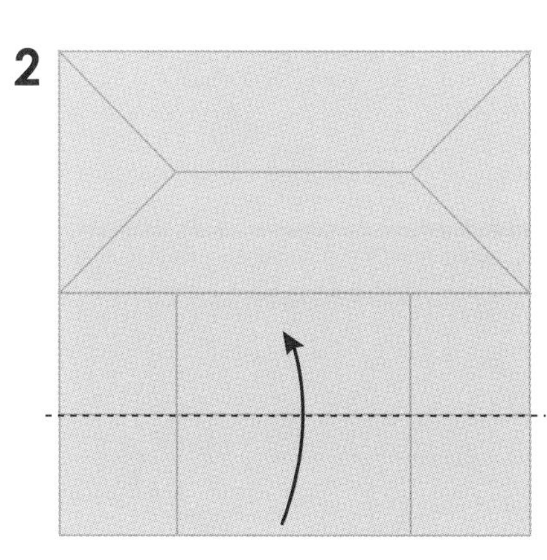

TEAR OFF COLORED SHEET ALONG THIS EDGE

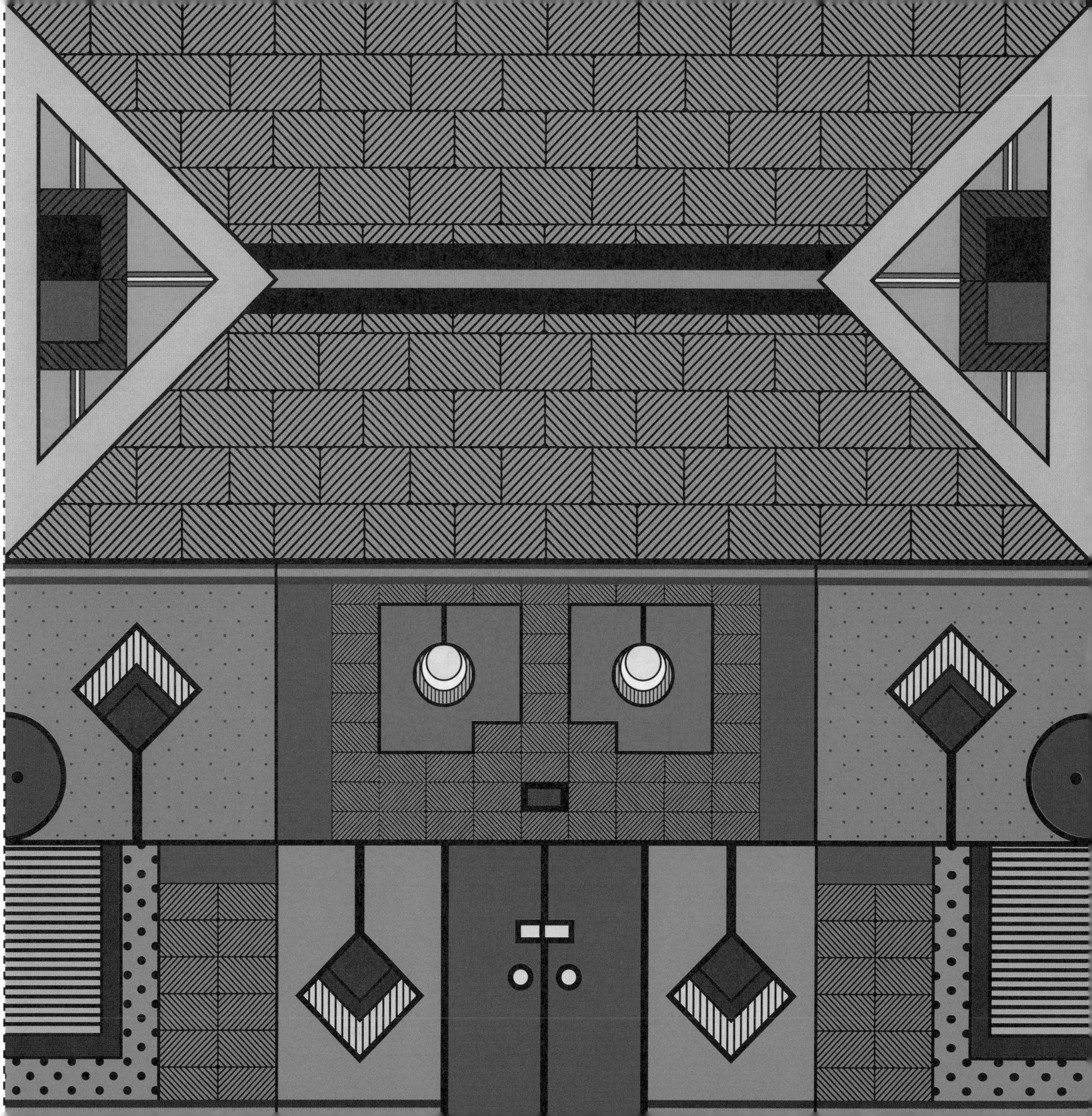

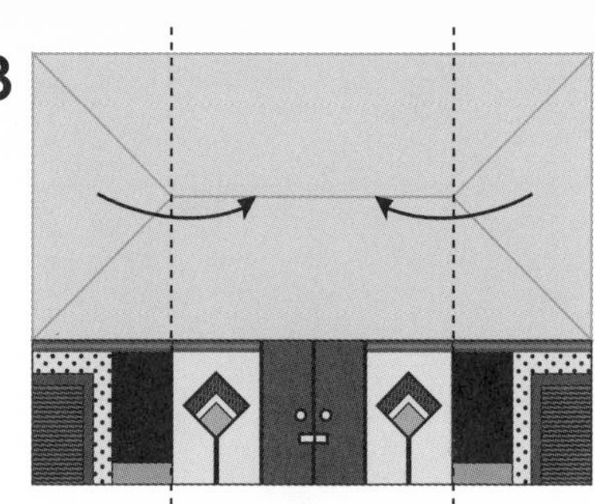

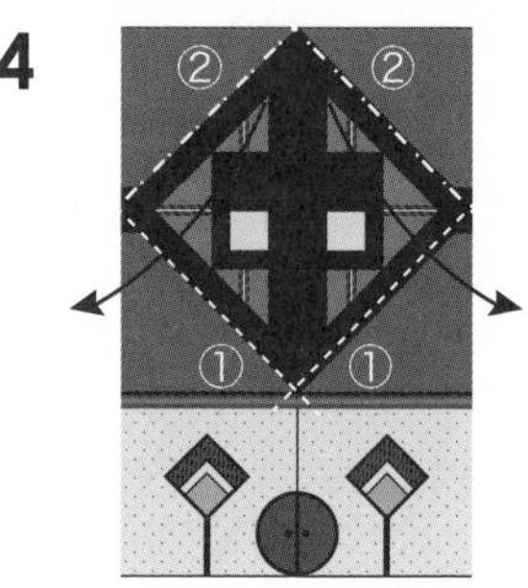

Valley fold at 1. Then press down while opening at 2.

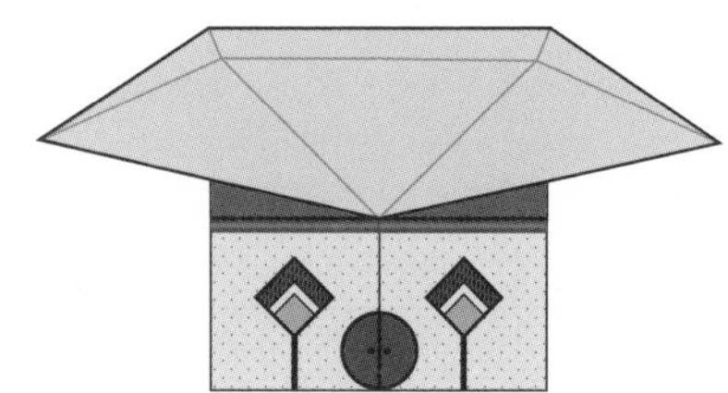

5

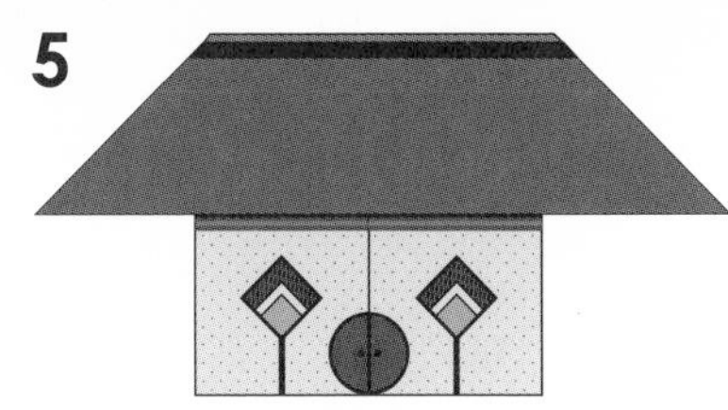

Open the doors at the front to reveal the interior of the house.

TEAR OFF COLORED SHEET ALONG THIS EDGE

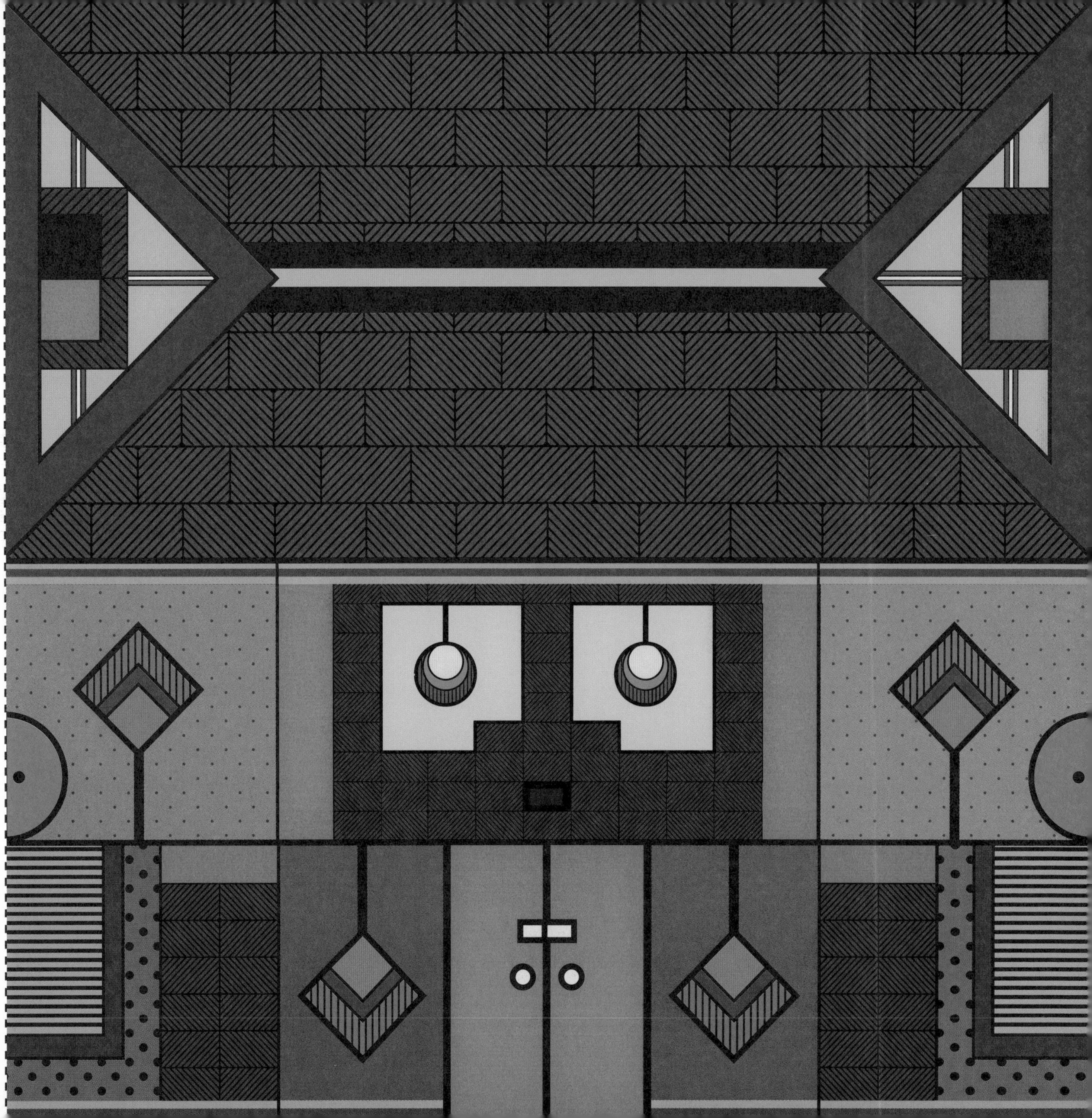

ハラペコカラス

HUNGRY CROW
(Harapeko-karasu)

As shown in the photo, as you hold both sides and alternately pull apart and push together, the crow's mouth will open and close as if eating. What will it catch? It's fun to hold a card in its mouth to use as a nametag, or to pass messages back and forth.

TEAR OFF COLORED SHEET ALONG THIS EDGE

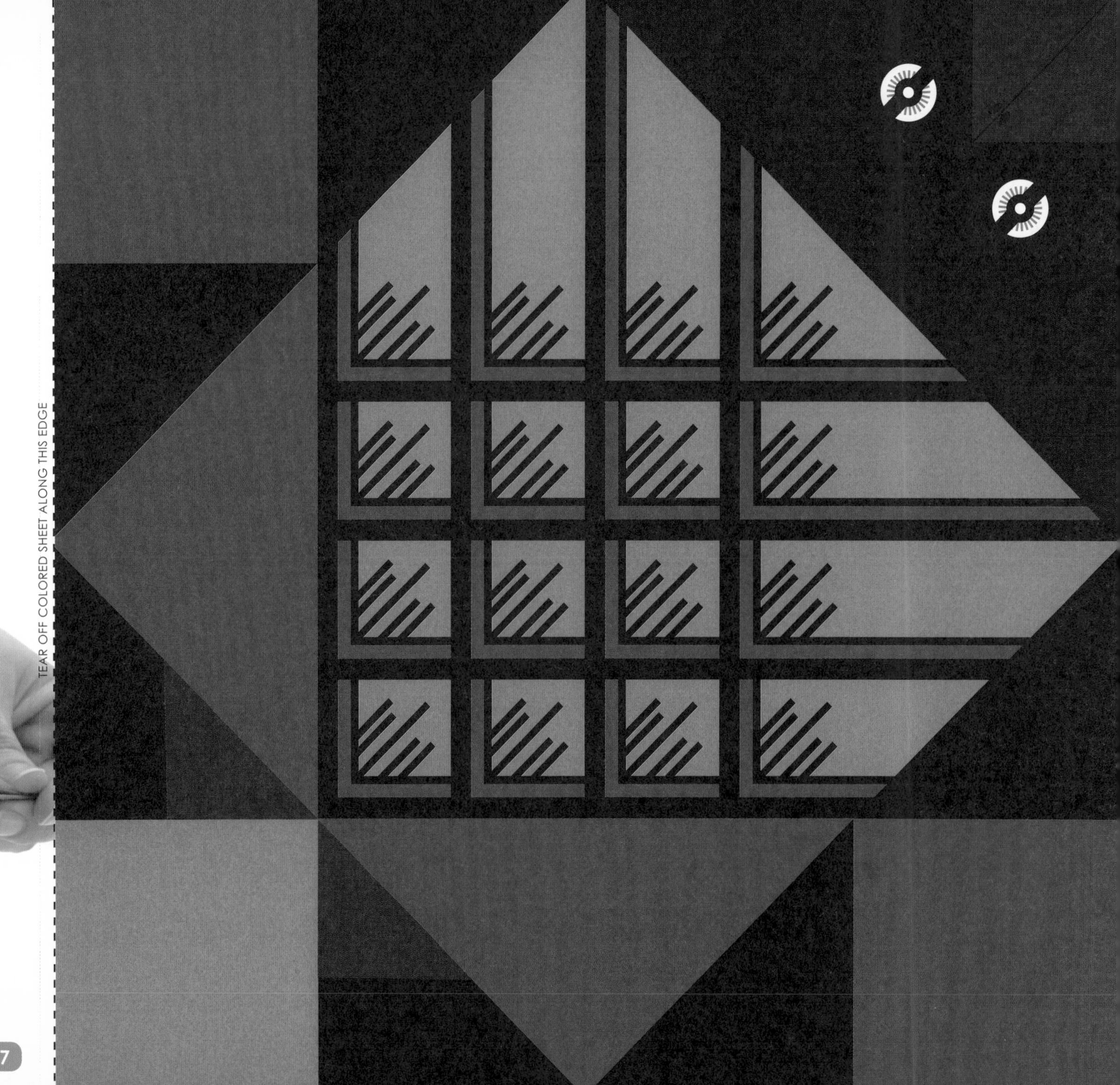

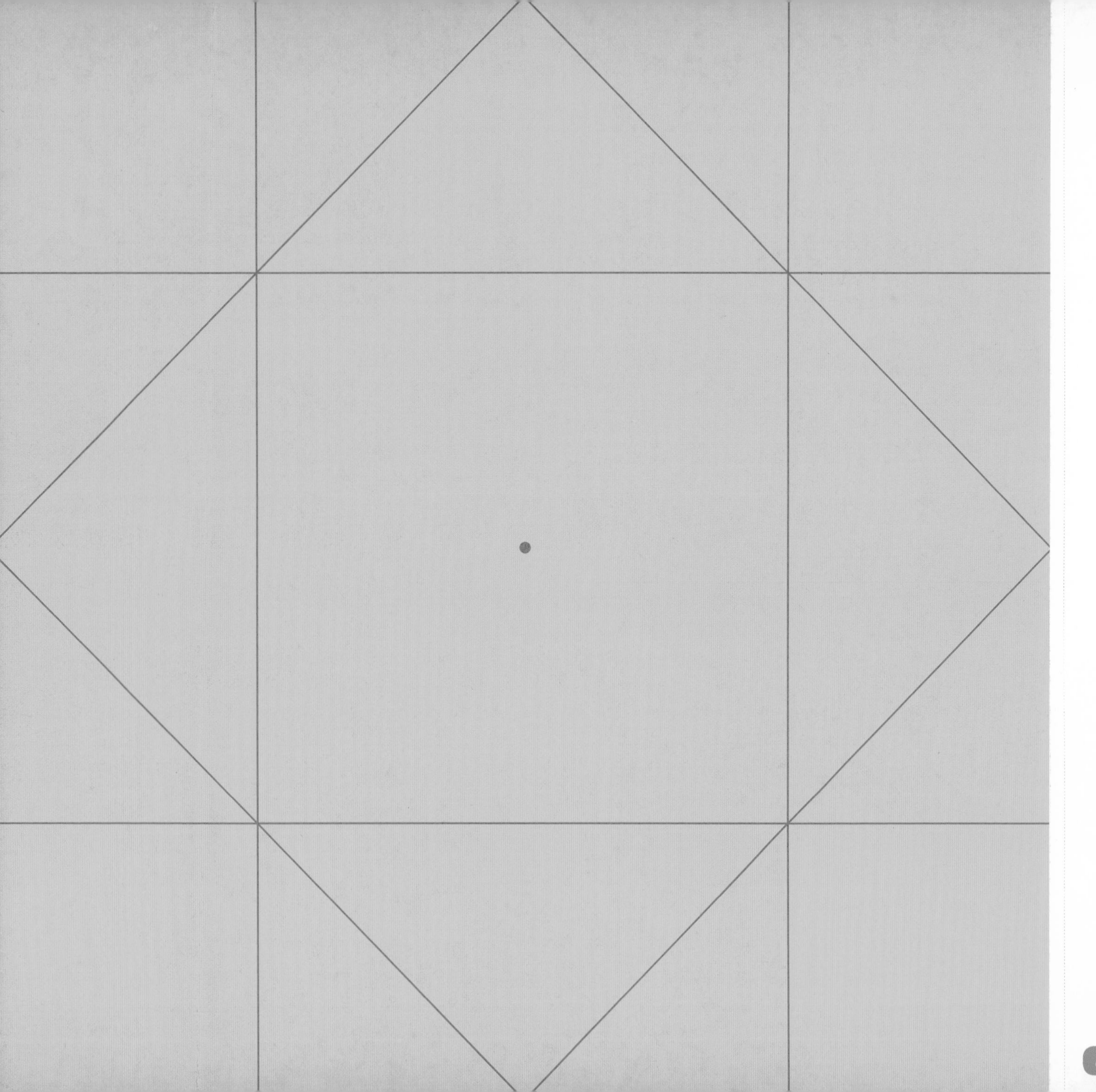

1

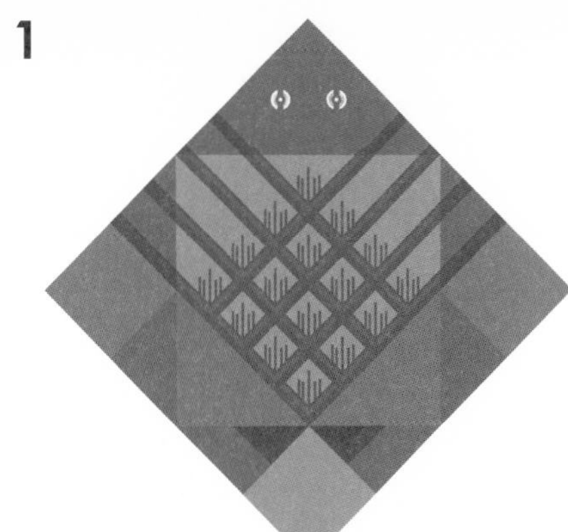

Turn over.

2

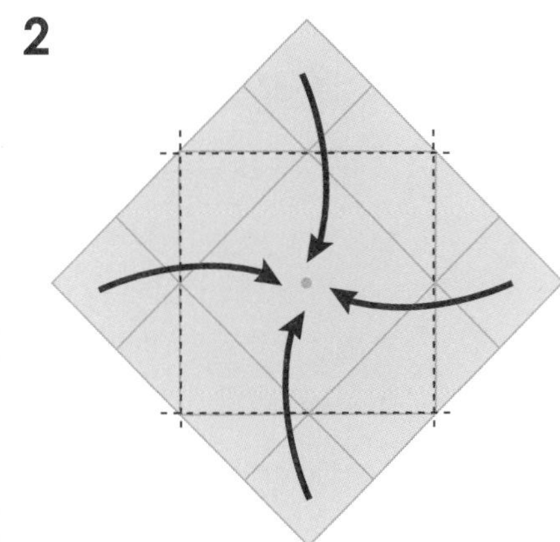

Valley fold all four corners to meet at the center point.

Turn over.

TEAR OFF COLORED SHEET ALONG THIS EDGE

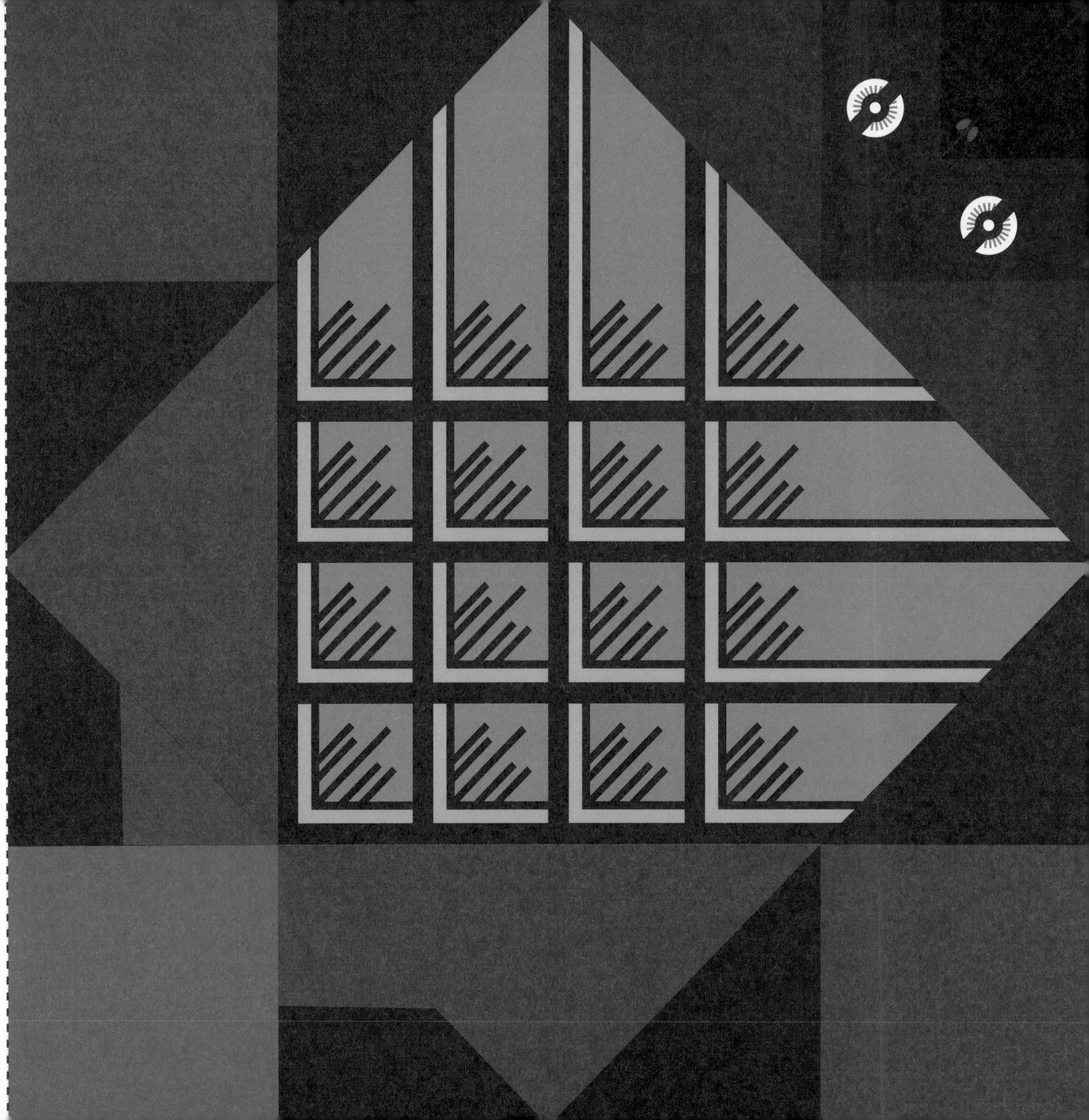

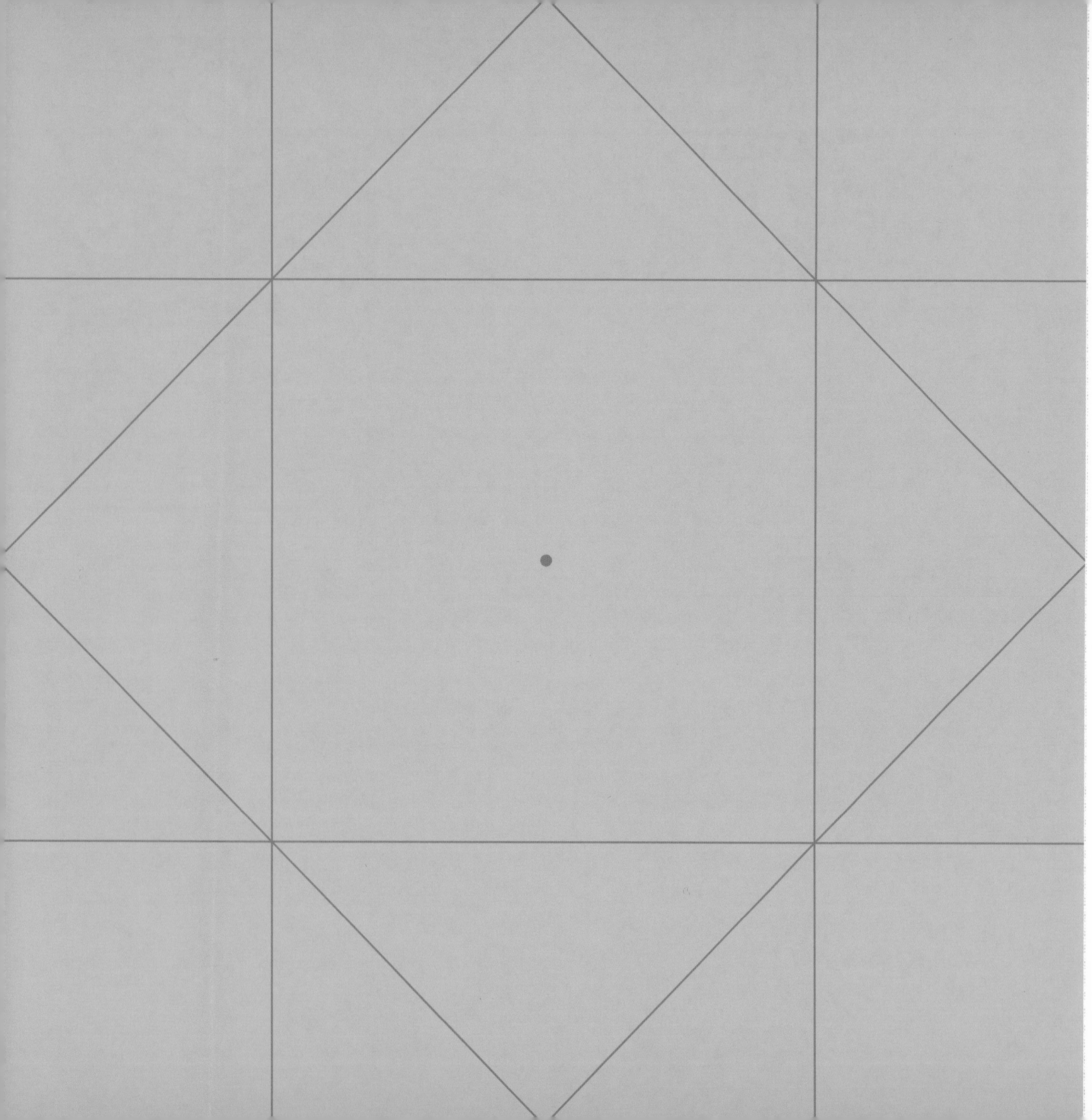

3

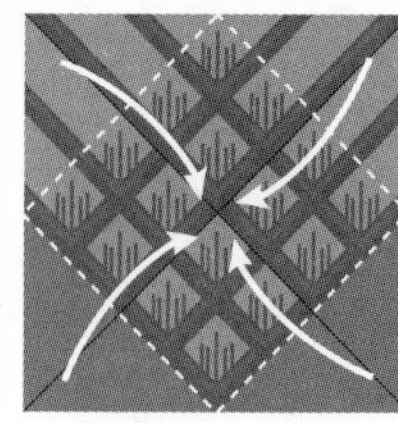

Valley fold all four corners to meet at the center point.

4

Turn over.

5

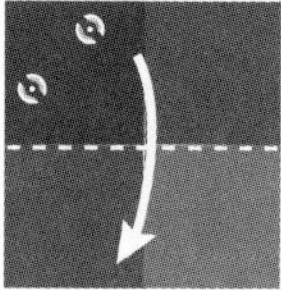

Fold in half.

6

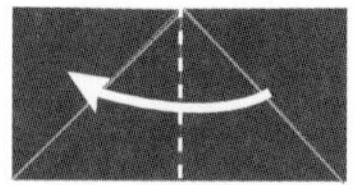

Fold in half again.

7

Pull open the inside as you press down.

8

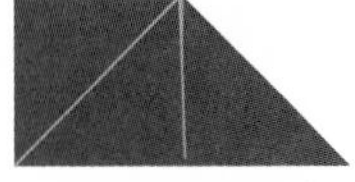

Turn over.

9

Pull open the inside as you press down.

10

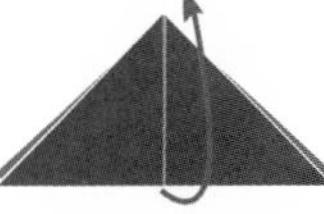

Open and spread.

TEAR OFF COLORED SHEET ALONG THIS EDGE

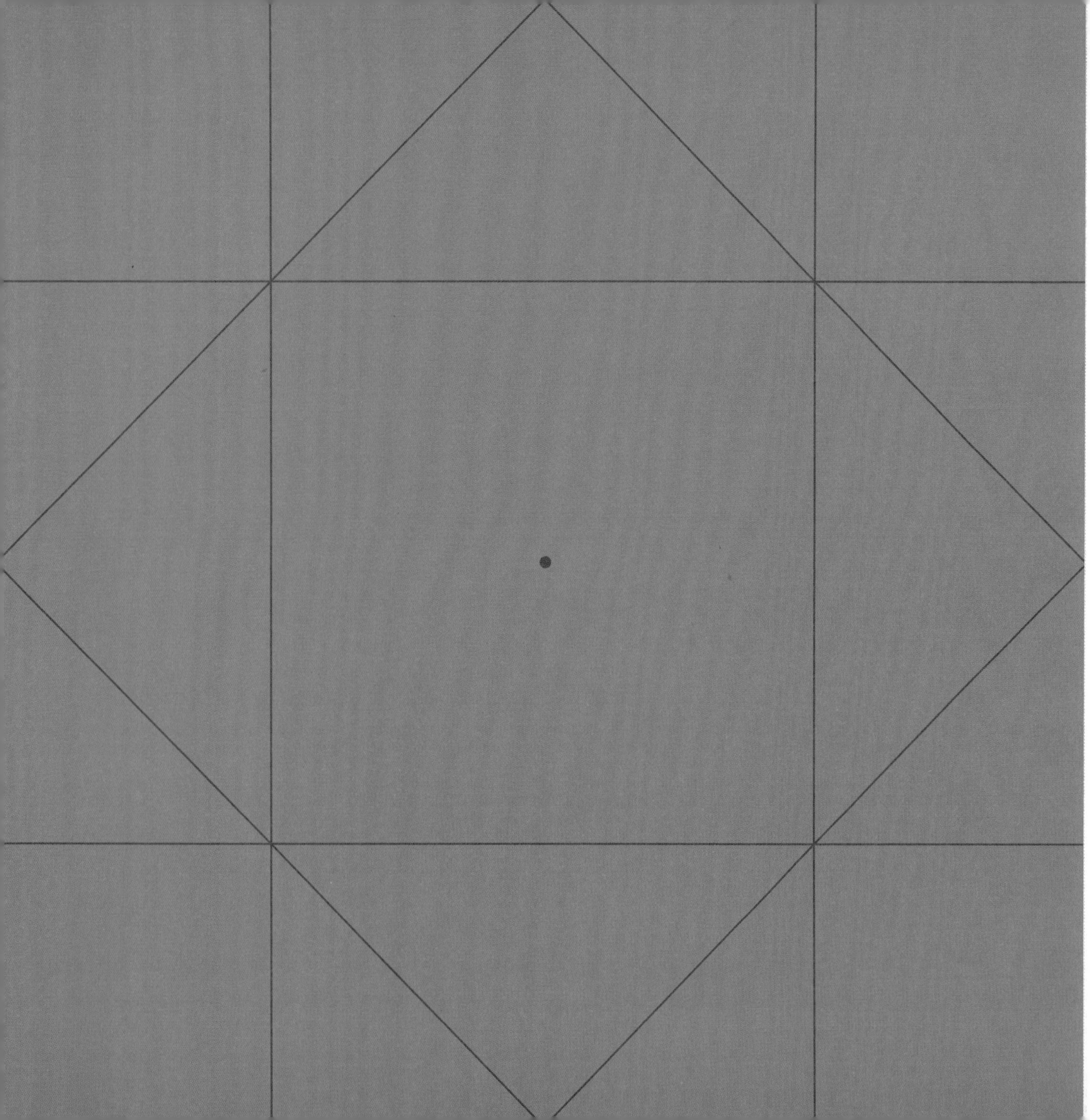

11

Pinch and push in the interior corners to puff up the body.

Tug back and forth as shown and watch the crow squawk with its beak!

カエル

LEAPING FROG
(Kaeru)

Push the frog's bottom down using your index finger, give it a good snap, and the frog will leap away! Put some obstacles in front and try to make the frog jump over them. Make different-colored frogs and have a contest to see which one leaps the farthest.

TEAR OFF COLORED SHEET ALONG THIS EDGE

1
Turn over.
2
3
Make creases as shown.
TEAR OFF COLORED SHEET ALONG THIS EDGE

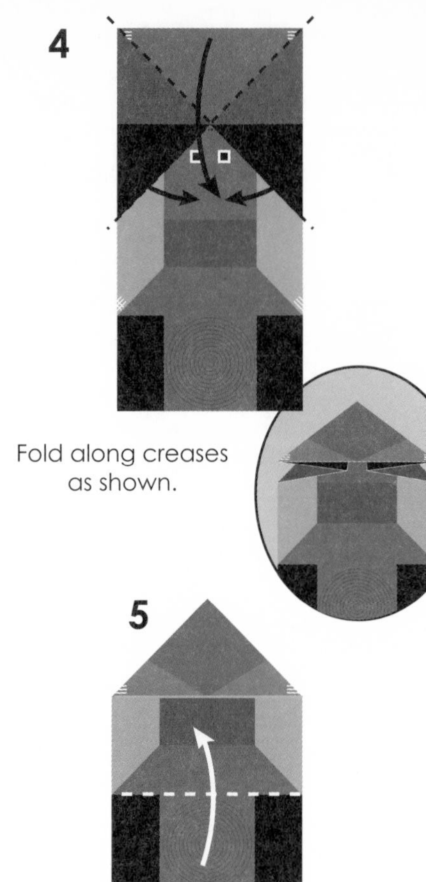

4

Fold along creases as shown.

5

Fold up and align to the edge.

6

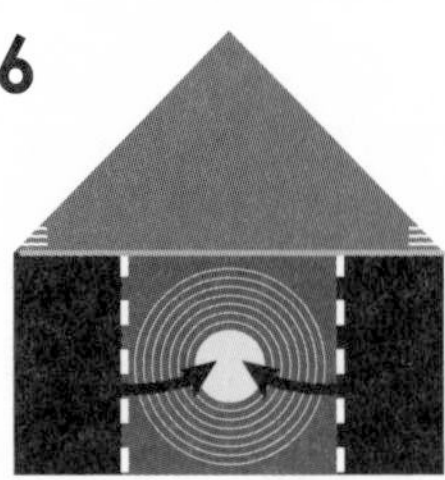

Valley fold bottom flaps to meet in the center.

7
8
Make a crease as shown.
9
Using the crease, open up as you press down.
10
Fold corners up.
TEAR OFF COLORED SHEET ALONG THIS EDGE

11

12

13

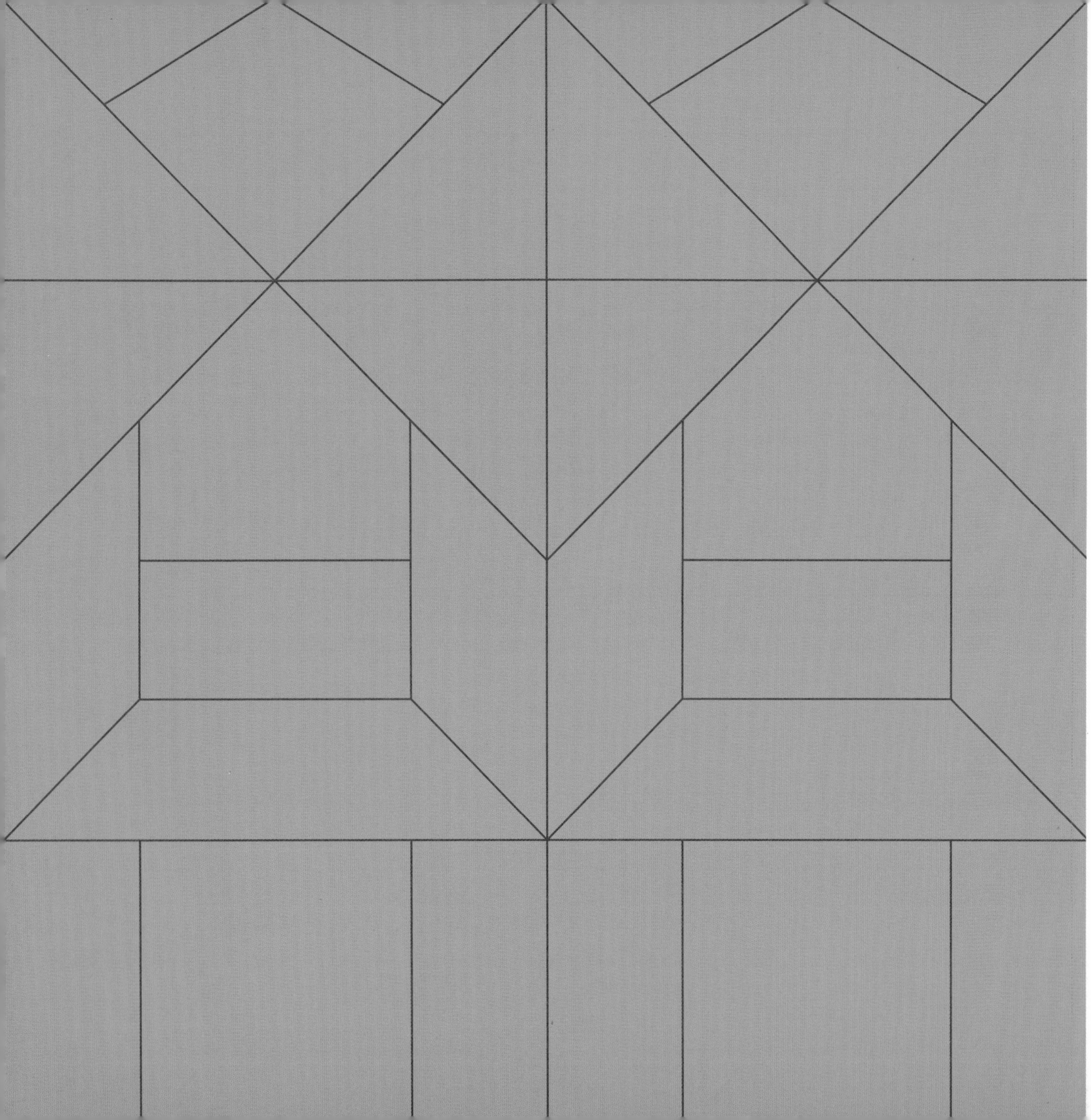

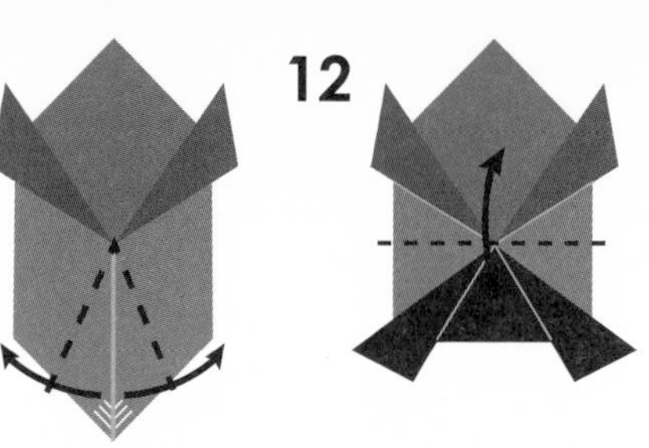

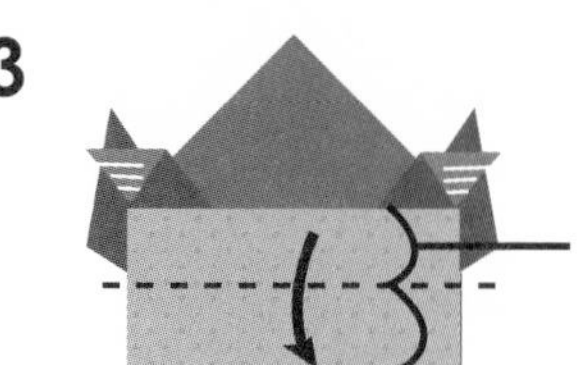

Make a narrow valley fold.

14

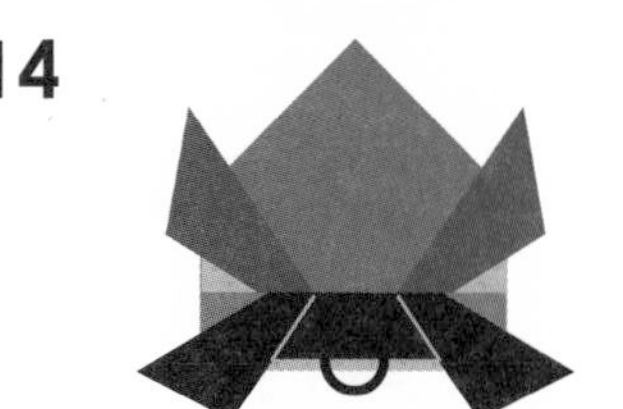

Open slightly at circled area.

15

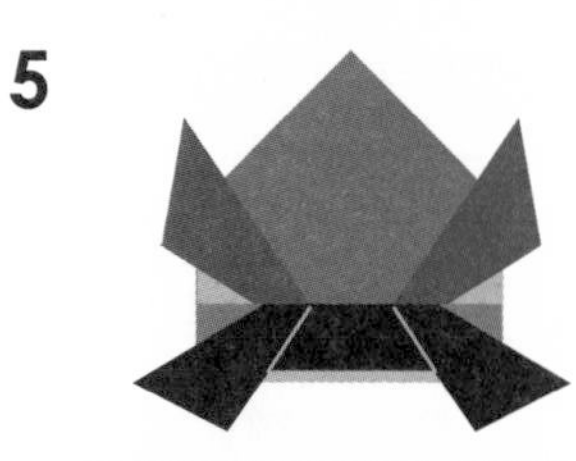

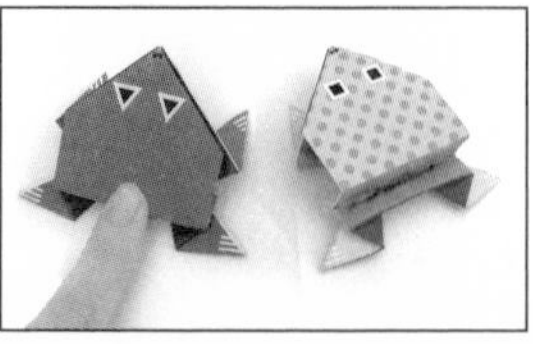

Turn over. Press down on the frog's rear end, let it snap free, and watch the frog jump! Fold using the opposite side and your frog will be another color!

ハト

PIGEON
(Hato)

As shown in the photo, hold the back using your index and middle fingers, then push forward and release to make it fly! How far will your pigeon soar? The person who makes the pigeon fly the farthest wins.

TEAR OFF COLORED SHEET ALONG THIS EDGE

1

Turn over.

2

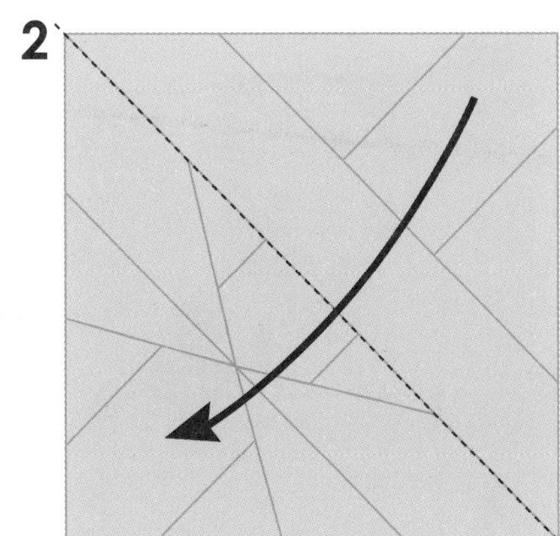

TEAR OFF COLORED SHEET ALONG THIS EDGE

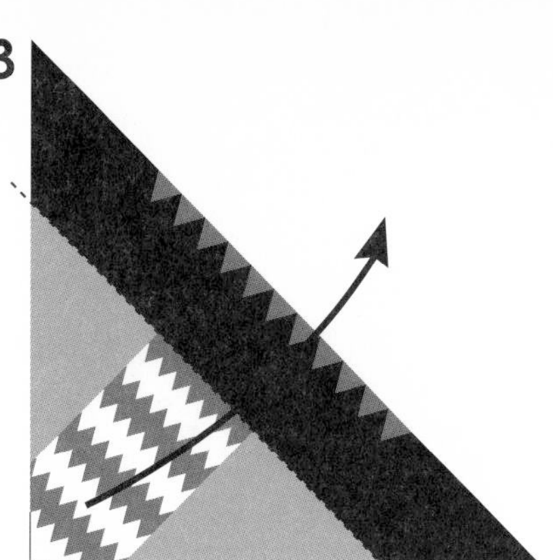

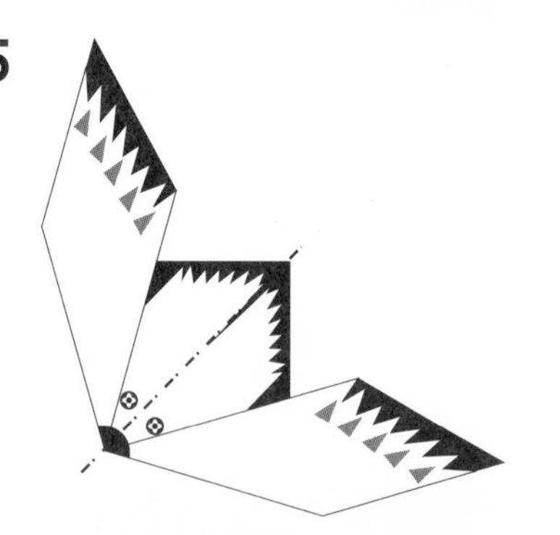

Mountain fold in half.

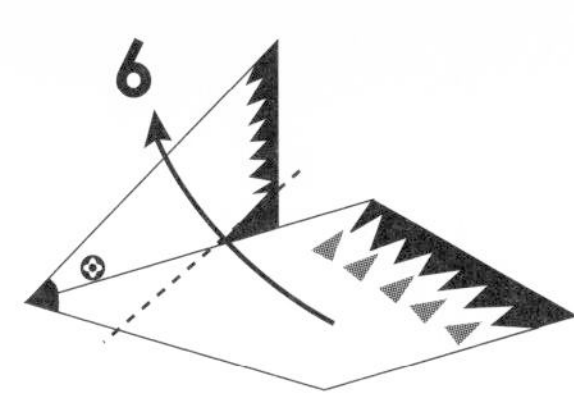

Valley fold to spread the wing. Do the same on the reverse.

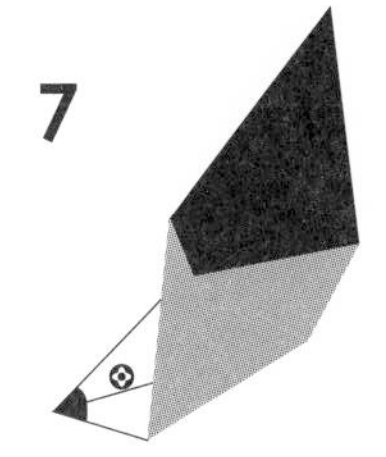

With the wings flat, hold as shown and push off to make it fly!

TEAR OFF COLORED SHEET ALONG THIS EDGE

カザグルマ

PINWHEEL
(Kazaguruma)

Attach the pinwheel to a small stick, then blow on it to make it turn, or put it outside and let it catch the wind. Will it spin around? Which way is the wind blowing today?

TEAR OFF COLORED SHEET ALONG THIS EDGE

1

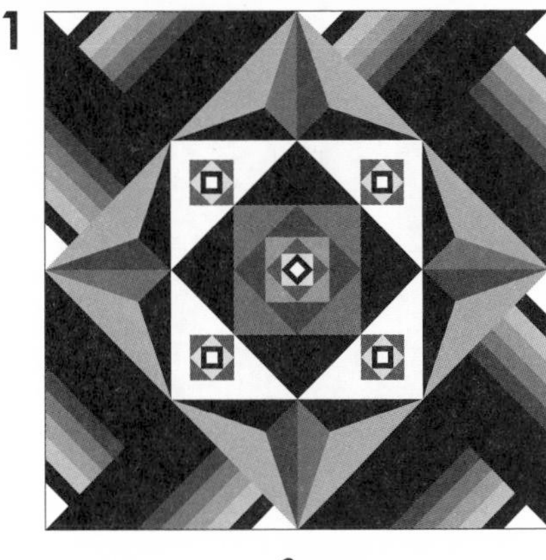

Turn over.

2

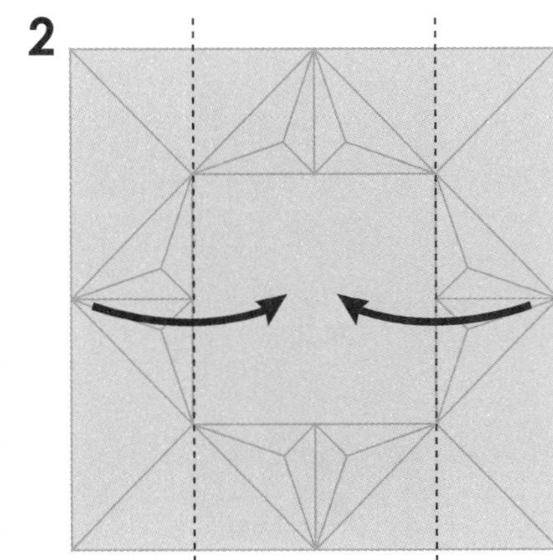

TEAR OFF COLORED SHEET ALONG THIS EDGE

3

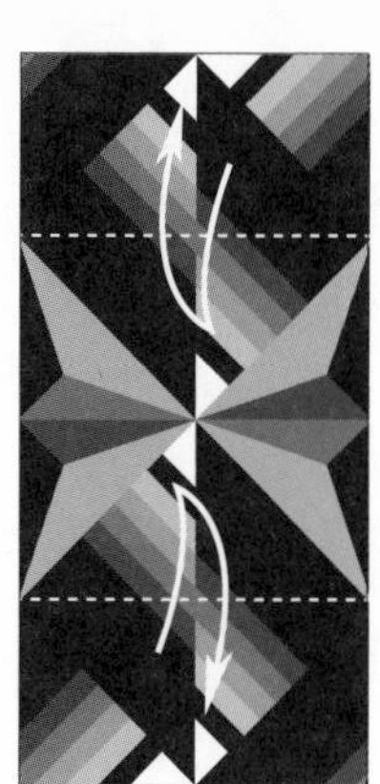

Make creases as shown.

4

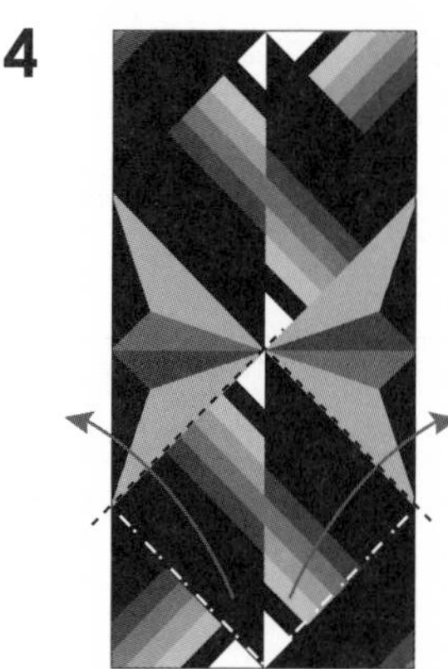

Using the creases, pull open the lower corners as you press down.

5

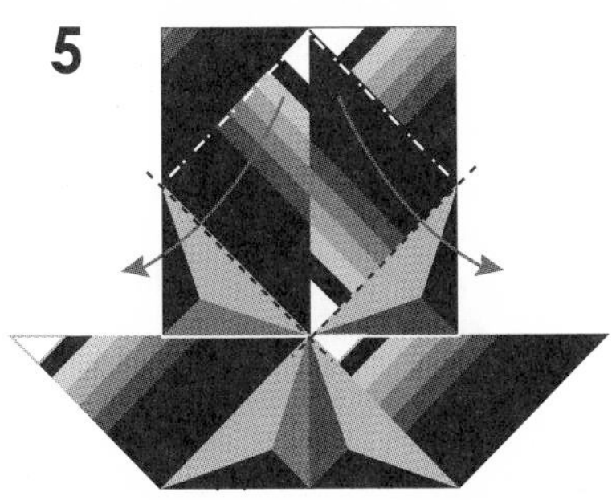

Repeat step 4 at the opposite end.

6

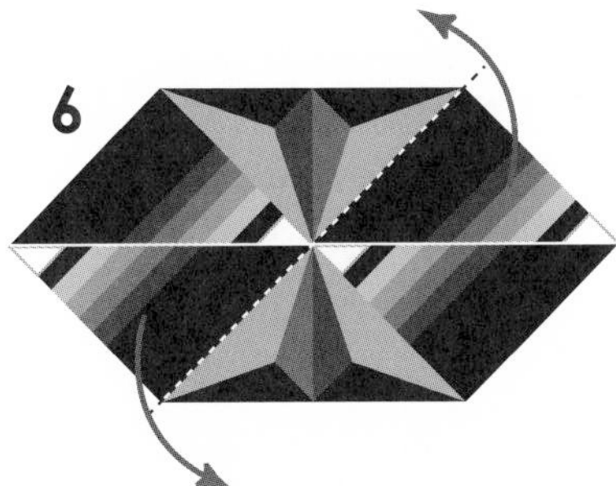

Valley fold flaps as shown to create the pinwheel star.

TEAR OFF COLORED SHEET ALONG THIS EDGE

Use a pin to make a hole in the back, insert a thin stick, and watch the wind make your pinwheel spin!

クルクルチョウ

SPINNING BUTTERFLY *(Kurukuru-cho)*

Holding the tail as shown in the photo, lift up the butterfly and let go. Watch it spin and spiral as it flutters to the ground. Gently catch it on the way down. Try releasing two butterflies at once. Which one will spin its wings the fastest?

TEAR OFF COLORED SHEET ALONG THIS EDGE

1

Turn over.

2

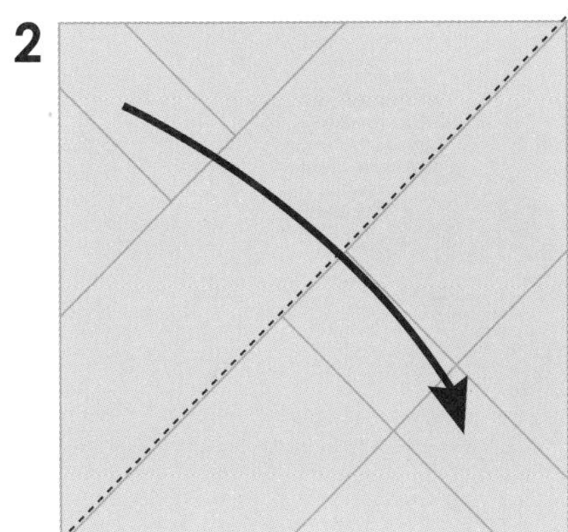

TEAR OFF COLORED SHEET ALONG THIS EDGE

3
4

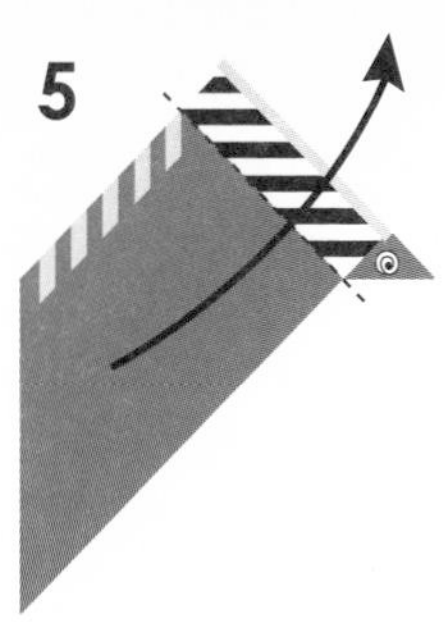

Valley fold to lift the wing away from the body. Do the same on the reverse.

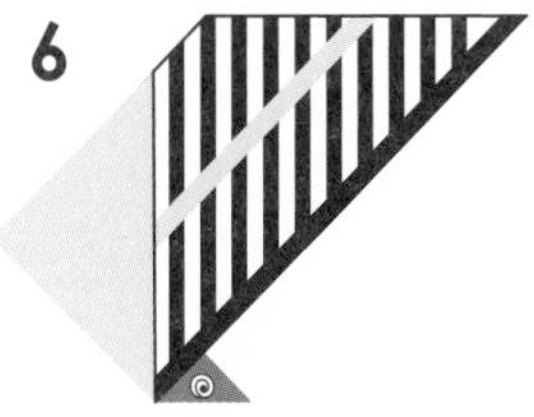

Keep the wings extended out flat and hold as shown. Let go and watch the butterfly whirl and flutter down!

TEAR OFF COLORED SHEET ALONG THIS EDGE

トントンスモウ

SUMO THUMPERS
(Tonton-sumo)

Make a *dohyo* (sumo fighting ring) using, for example, an upside-down box or a tabletop (see the backgrounds section for a printed *dohyo*). Send your origami sumo wrestlers into battle by lightly drumming on the edges of the box (or pounding on the table). If your wrestler falls down or falls off the dohyo, you lose. Who will be the *yokozuna* (grand champion)?

TEAR OFF COLORED SHEET ALONG THIS EDGE

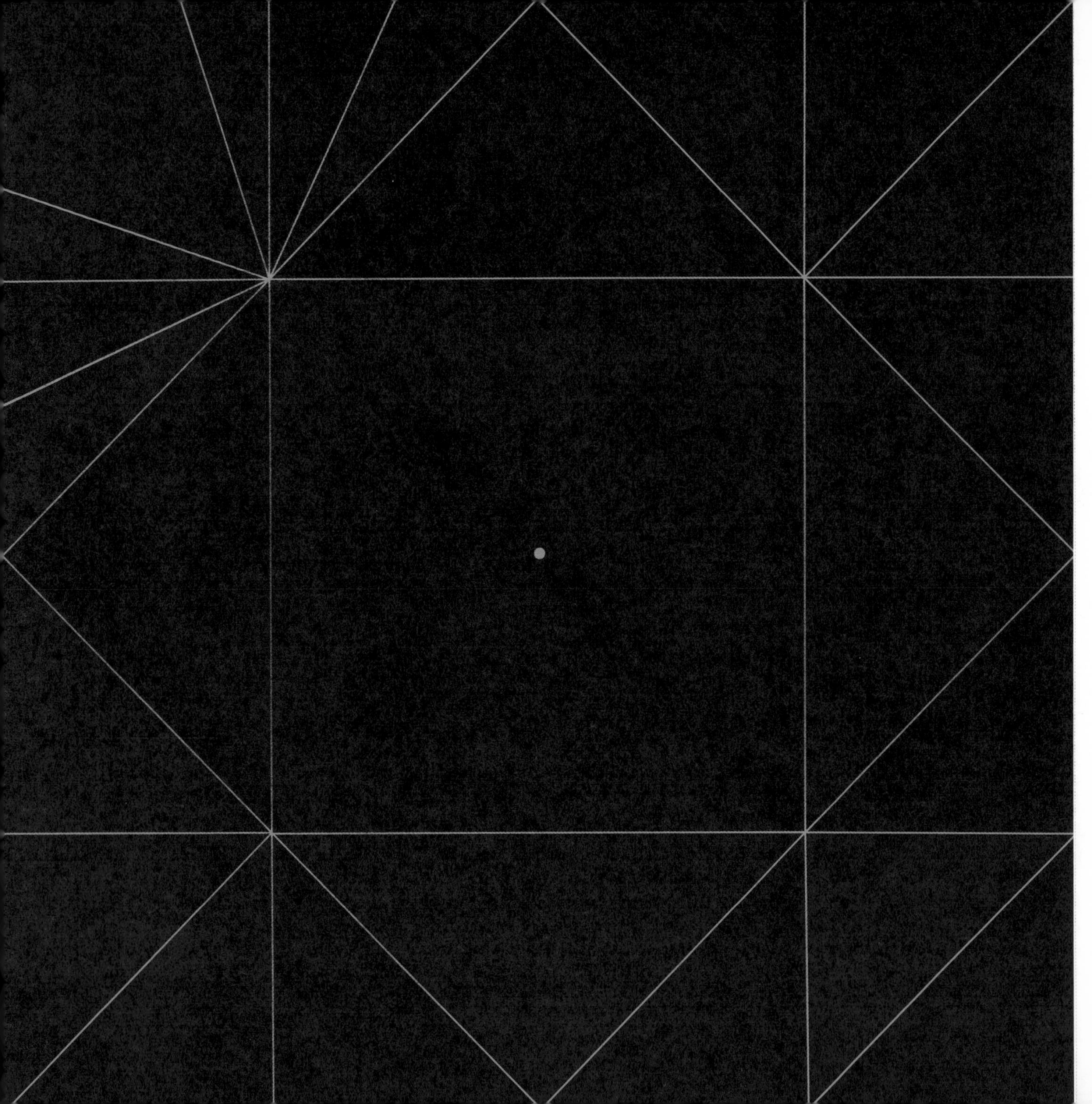

1

Turn over.

2

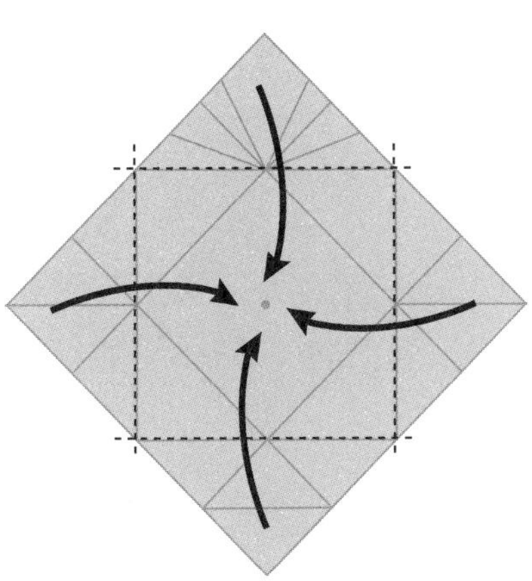

Fold in all four corners to meet at the center.

TEAR OFF COLORED SHEET ALONG THIS EDGE

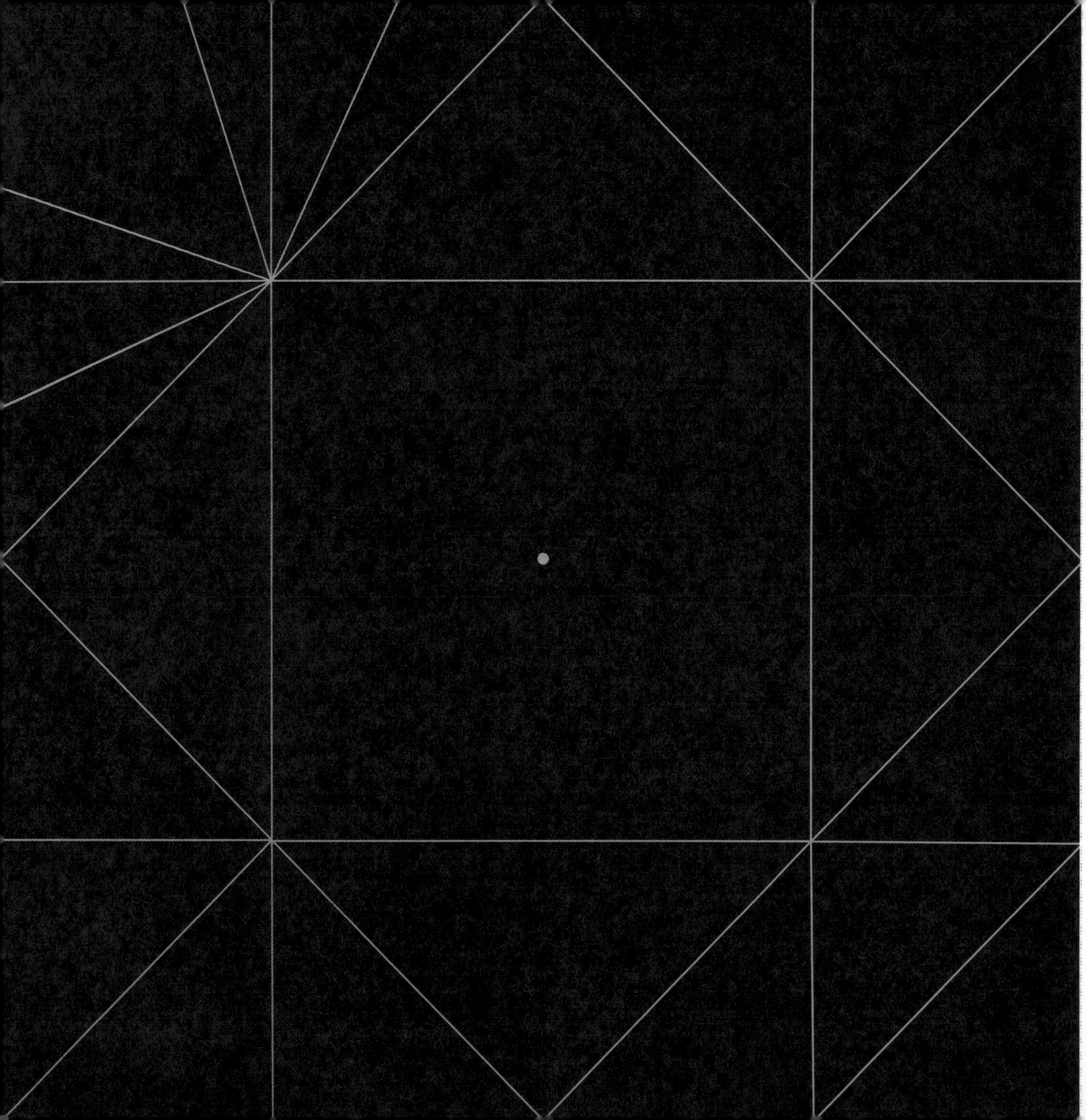

3

Fold in all four corners to meet at the center.

4

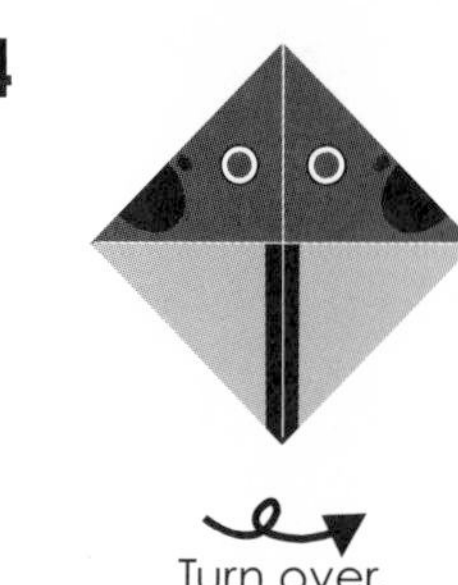

Turn over.

5

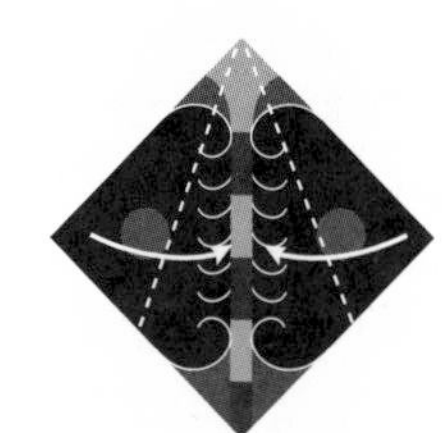

Valley fold the outer edges to meet along the vertical center line.

6

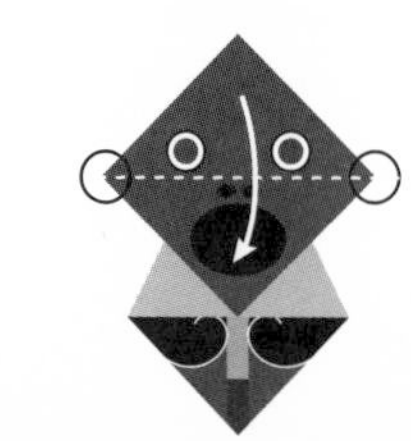

Pull out the corners from behind as shown and valley fold from the top down.

7

Turn over.

8

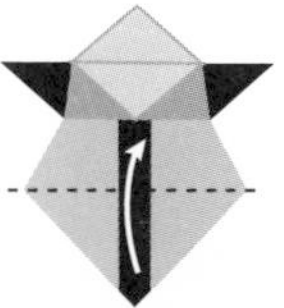

Valley fold as shown.

9

Fold and unfold the bottom edge to the upper left edge as shown to make a crease.

10

Repeat step 9 by folding and unfolding to the upper right edge.

11

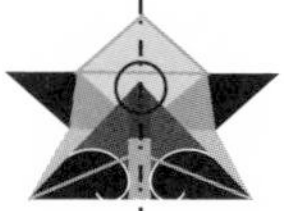

Using the creases, pinch the circled point and pull up into a mountain fold.

TEAR OFF COLORED SHEET ALONG THIS EDGE

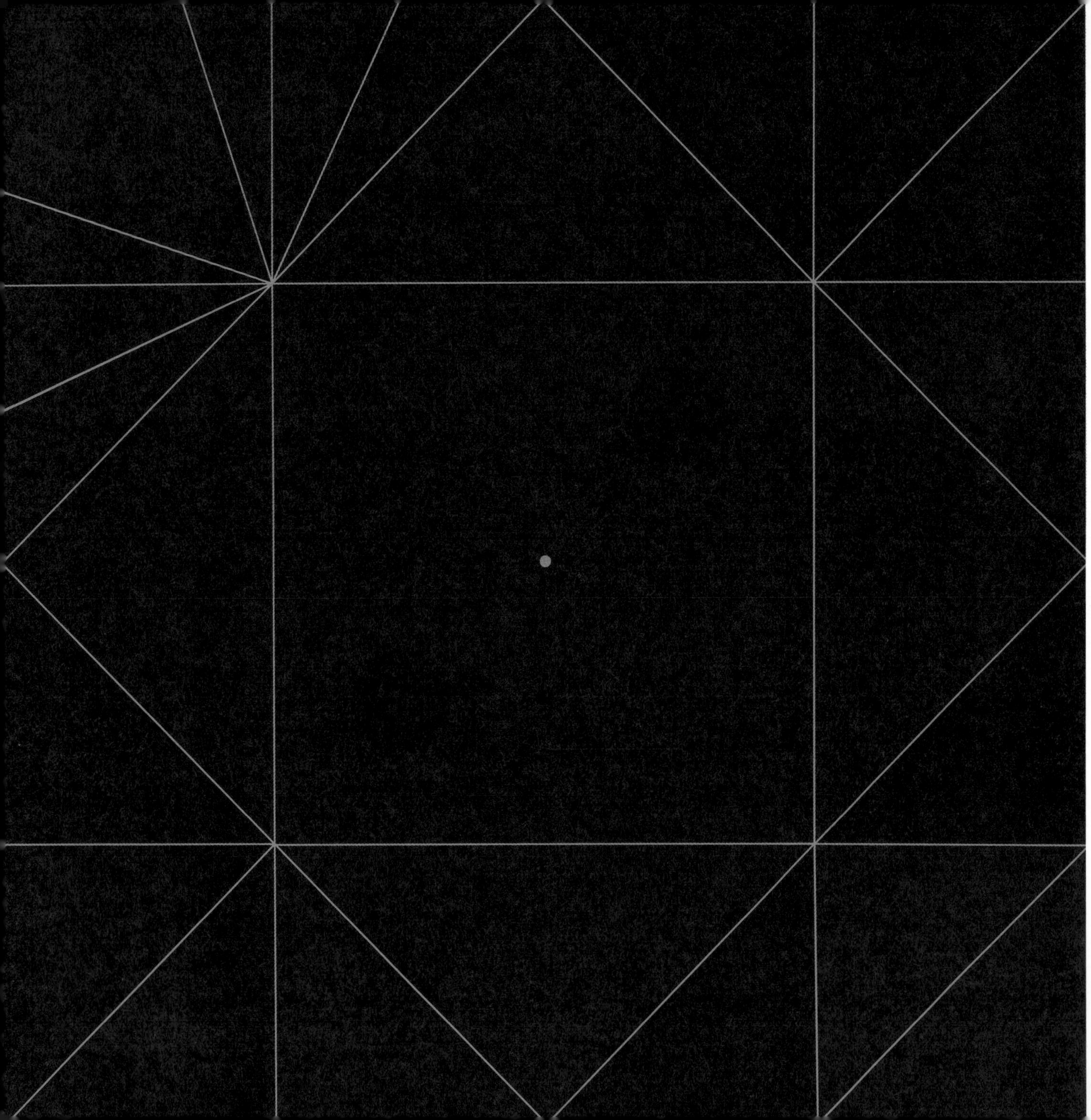

View from below.

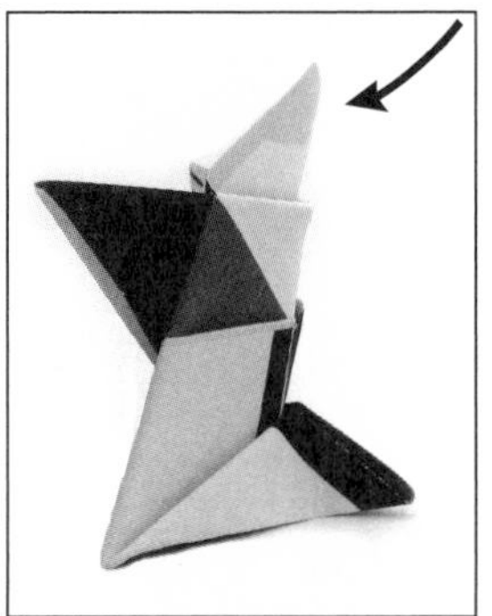

Insert your finger into the space behind the face and wiggle to puff up the figure.

Place two sumo wrestlers atop an empty box and draw a circle to make a sumo "ring." Use your fingertips to drum lightly on the box so that the surface vibrates and the wrestlers move. The first wrestler to fall down or move outside the ring loses the match!

シュリケン.1

THROWING STAR 1 (*Shuriken 1*) HALF A

You can use your origami paper to make a throwing star, or *shuriken*, just like the ninja use! As shown in the photo, hold the tip of the *shuriken* between your thumb and middle finger. Throw it by flipping your hand from back to front. But be careful: not to hit anyone! Combine this piece with HALF B (next project) to complete the throwing star.

TEAR OFF COLORED SHEET ALONG THIS EDGE

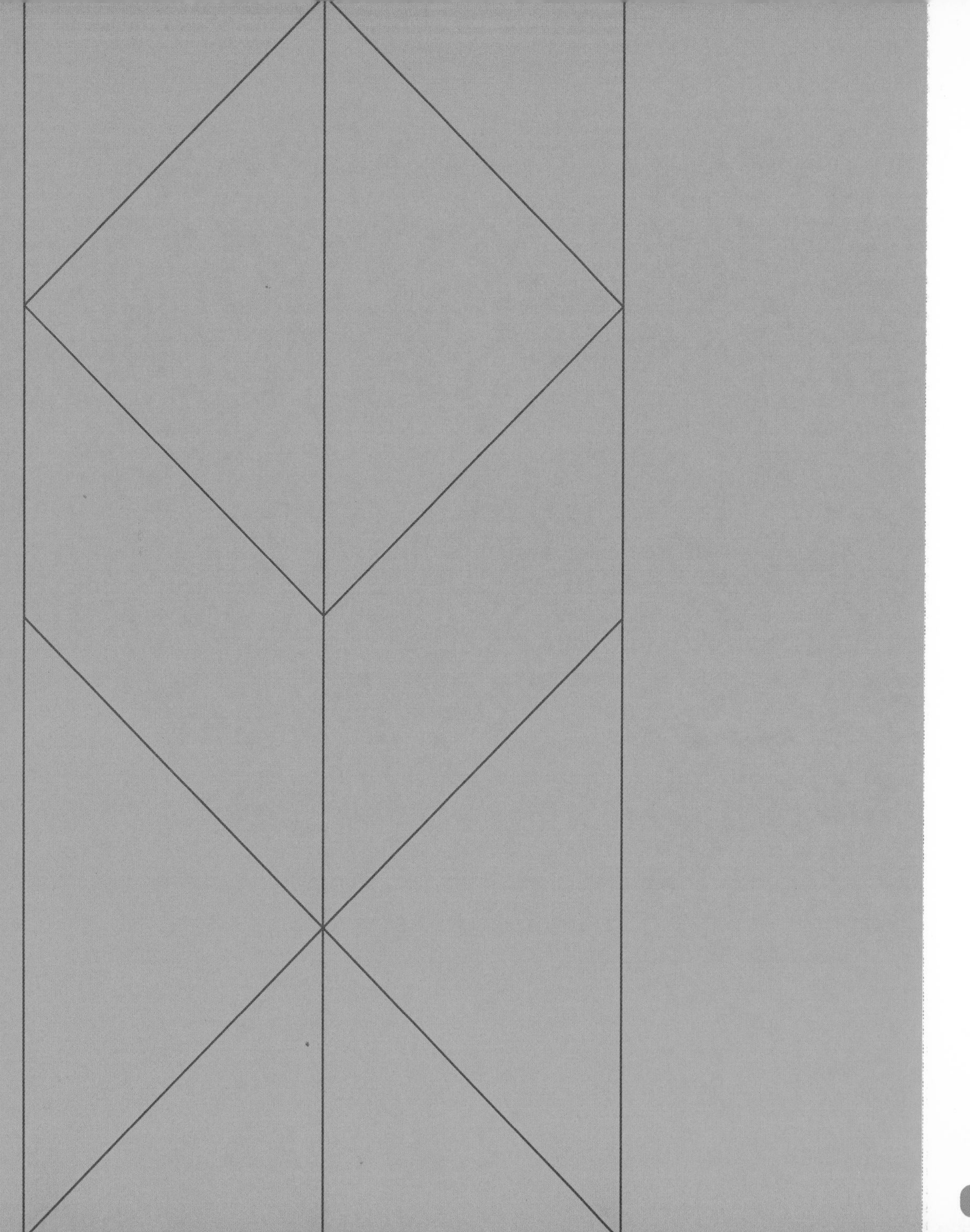

1

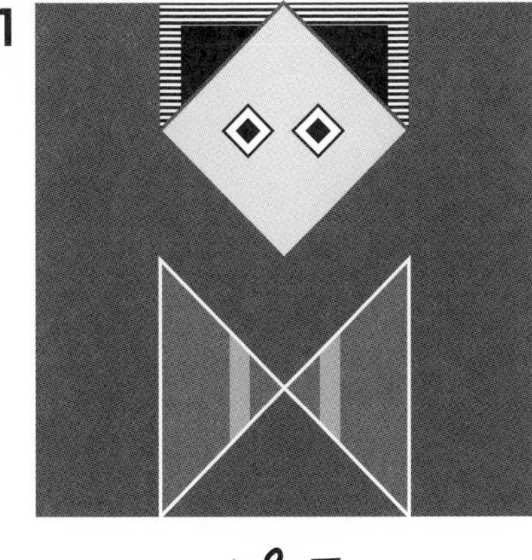

Turn over.

2

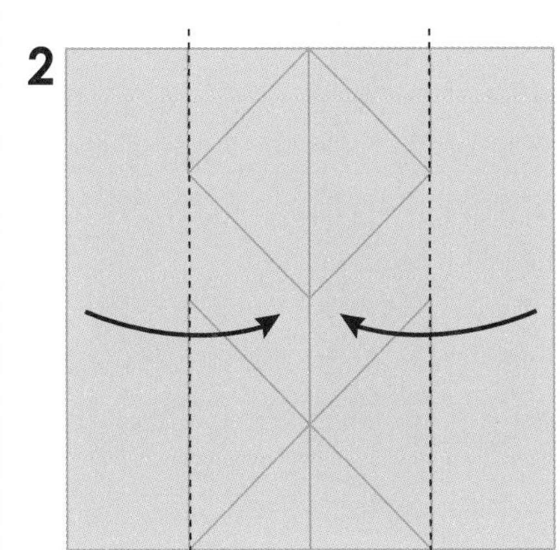

TEAR OFF COLORED SHEET ALONG THIS EDGE

3

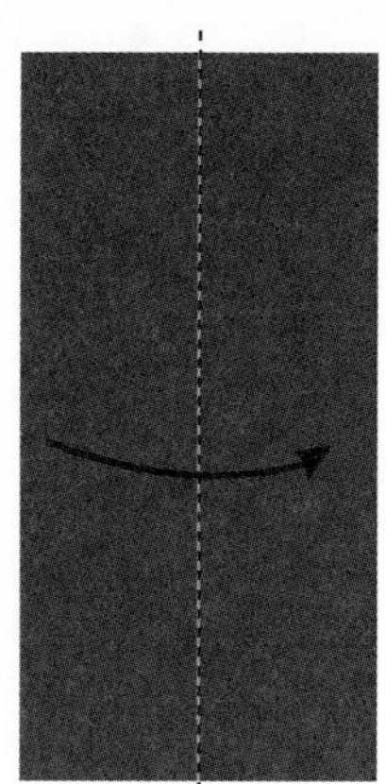

Valley fold in half.

4

Note the direction of the valley folds in steps 4–6.

5

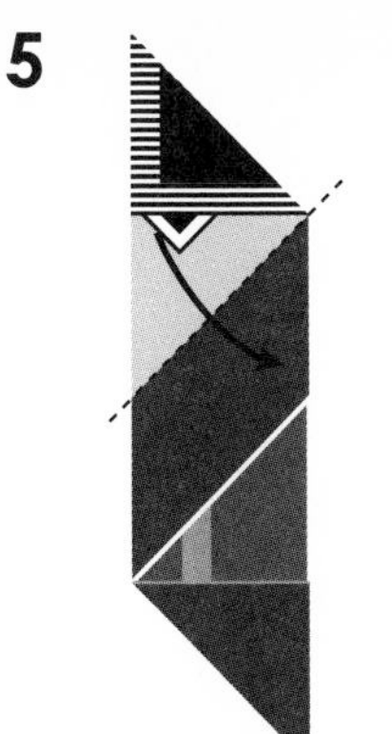

6

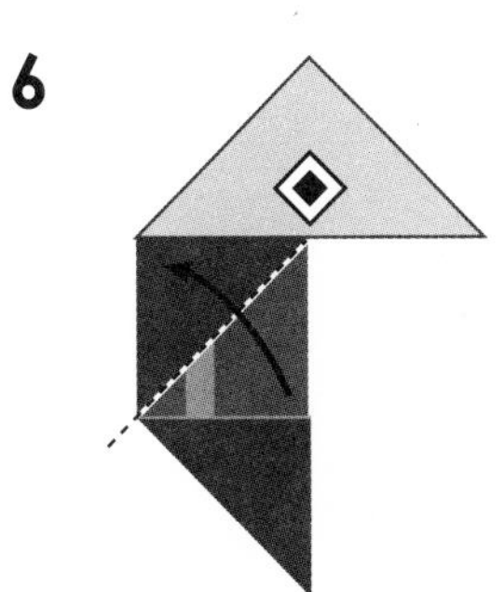

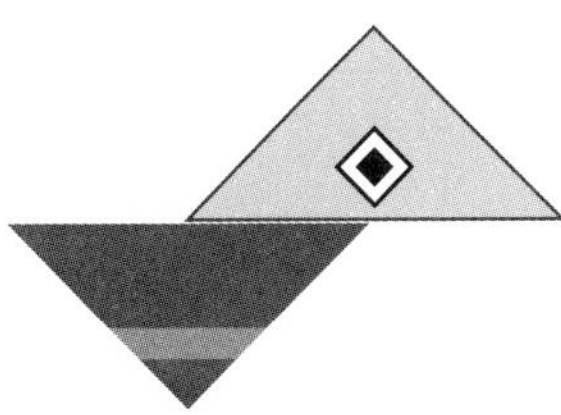

You will join this piece to HALF B to complete the throwing star.

TEAR OFF COLORED SHEET ALONG THIS EDGE

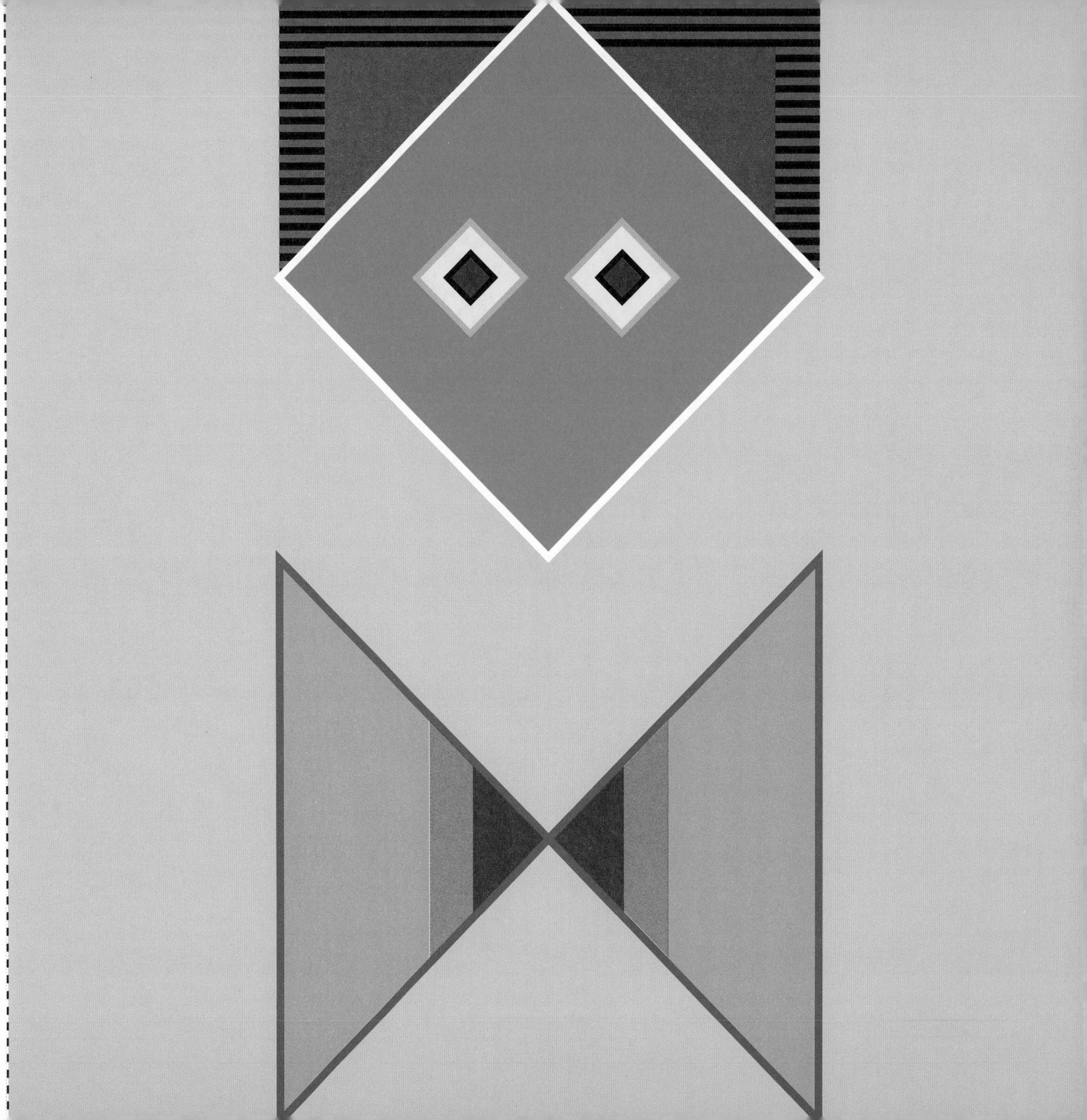

シュリケン.2

THROWING STAR 2 (*Shuriken 2*) HALF B

Use this with the preceding piece (HALF A) to complete the throwing star. As shown in the photo, hold the throwing star between two fingers of your closed fist. Now, practice an overhand throw for a different ninja technique!

TEAR OFF COLORED SHEET ALONG THIS EDGE

1
Turn over.
2
3
TEAR OFF COLORED SHEET ALONG THIS EDGE

4

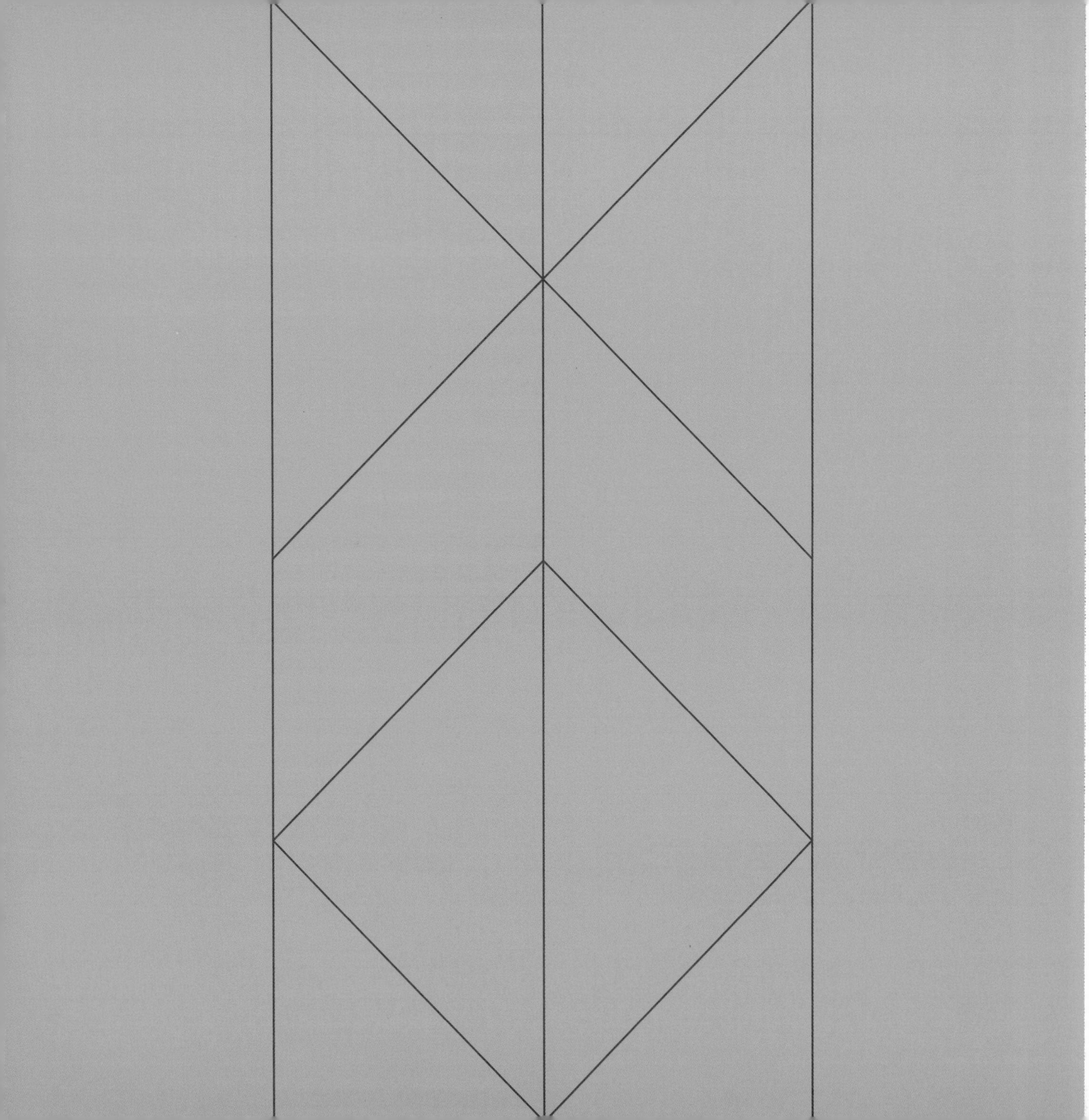

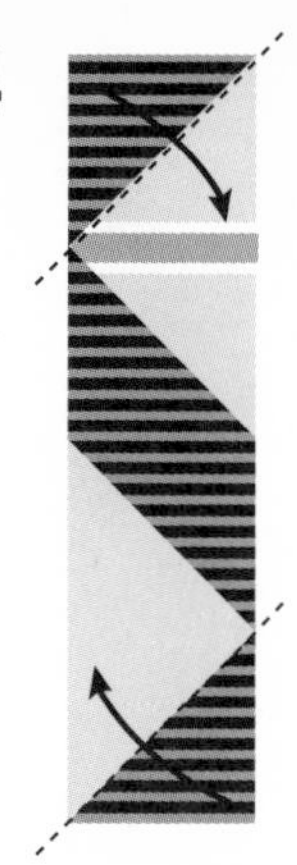

Note the direction of the valley folds in steps 4–6.

5

6

7

Turn over.

8

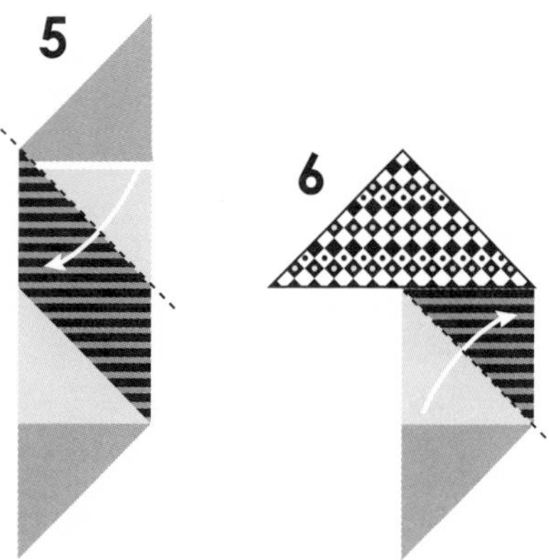

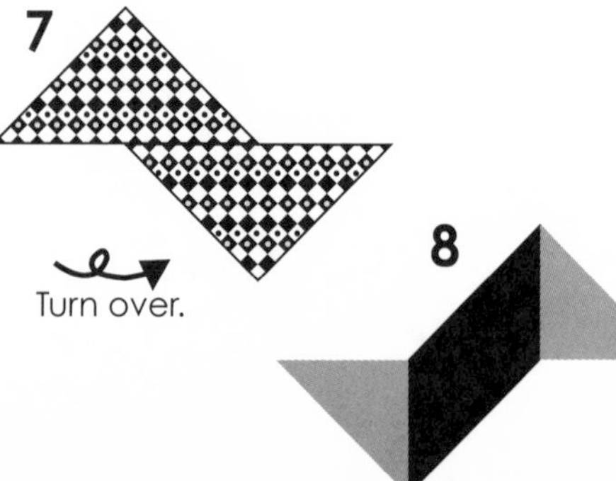

Now use the following steps to combine HALF A and HALF B.

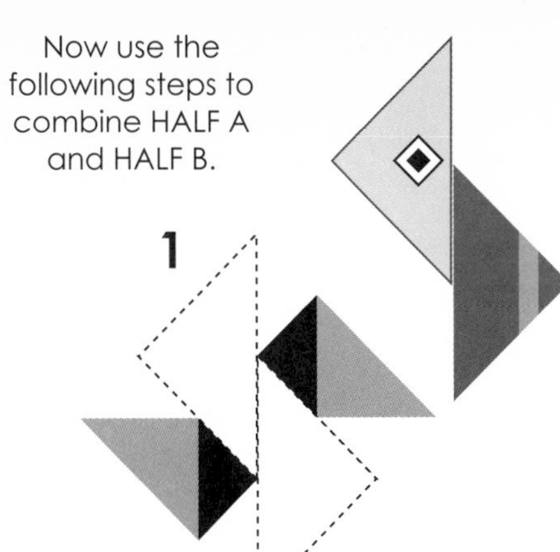
1

Stack HALF A and HALF B as shown.

2
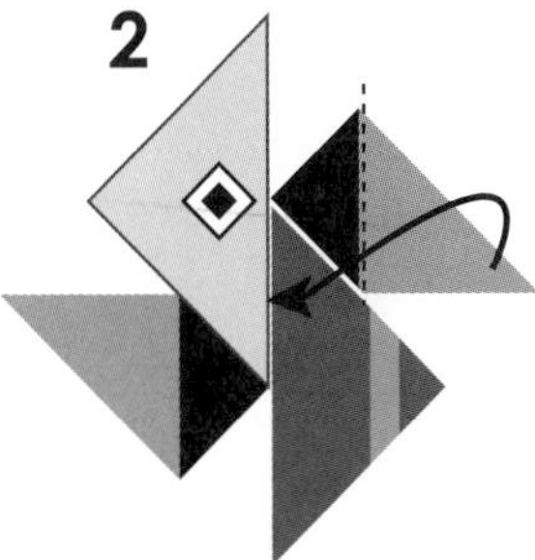

Fold and tuck one corner of HALF B into the interior pocket of HALF A as shown.

3
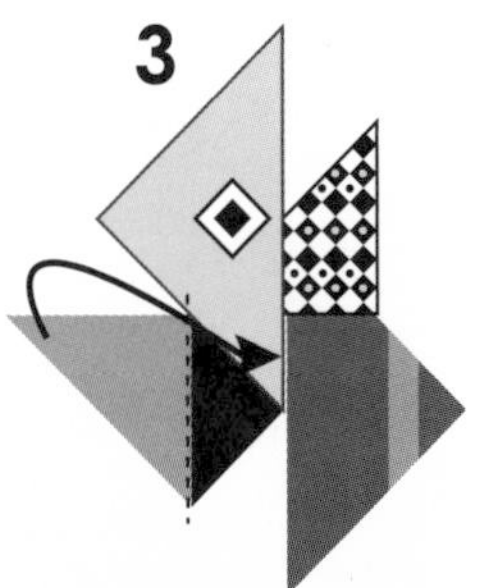

Now tuck the other corner of HALF B into the opposite interior pocket of HALF A as shown.

TEAR OFF COLORED SHEET ALONG THIS EDGE

4

Turn over.

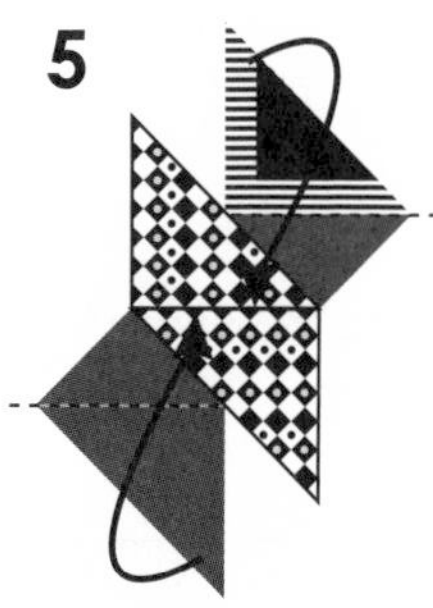

5

As in steps 2 and 3, tuck the loose corners into the open pockets as shown.

Hold the star between your fingers and throw; make like a ninja!

カッパ

WATER IMP
(Kappa)

A *kappa* is a Japanese water sprite—often quite mischievous! Holding the back as shown in the photo on page 119, alternatively pinch and release to open and close the *kappa*'s mouth! Your talking *kappa* is now complete! Have fun practicing your ventriloquist skills!

TEAR OFF COLORED SHEET ALONG THIS EDGE

1

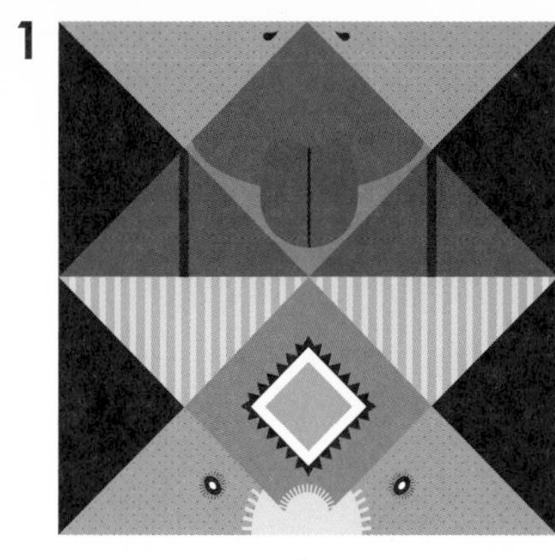

Turn over.

2

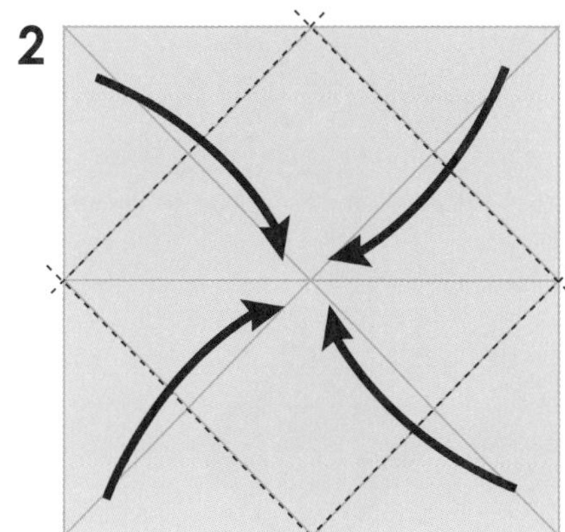

Valley fold all four corners to meet at the center.

TEAR OFF COLORED SHEET ALONG THIS EDGE

3

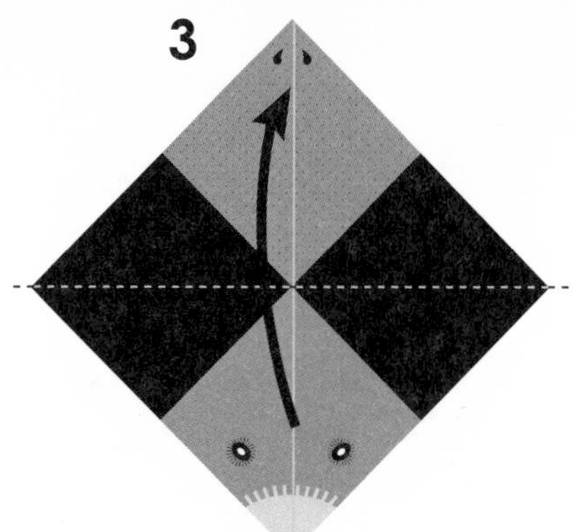

4

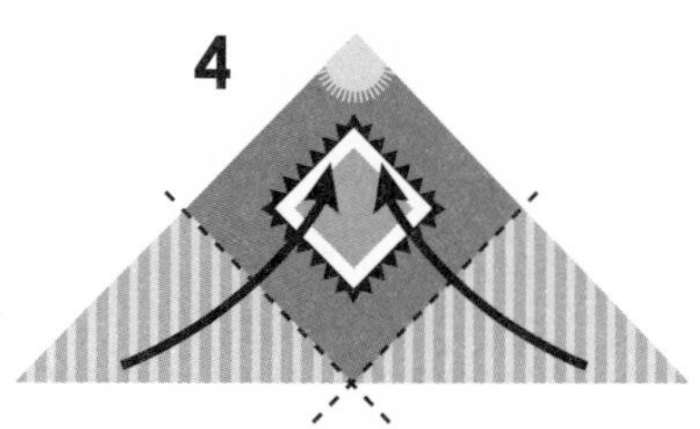

5

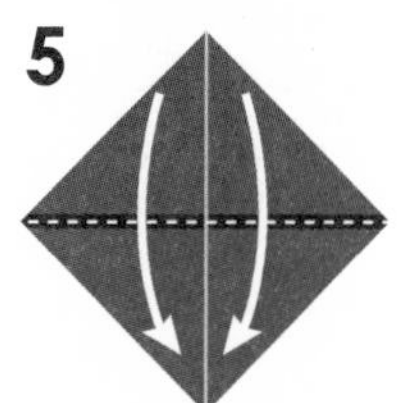

Fold down top layer.

6

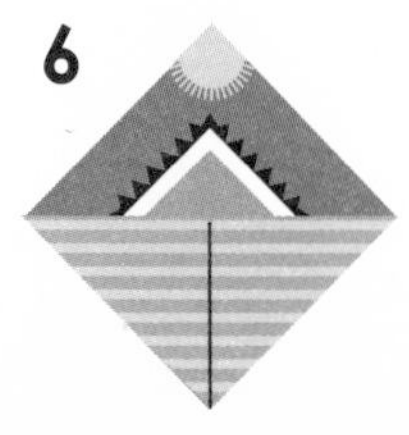

Turn over.

7

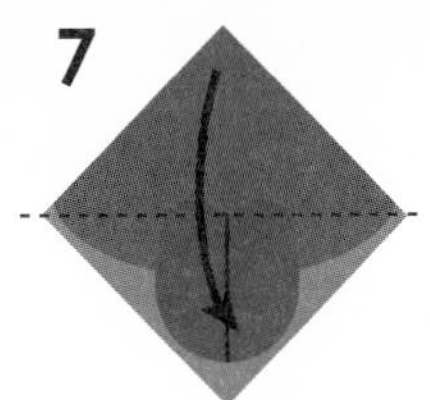

Fold down top layer.

8

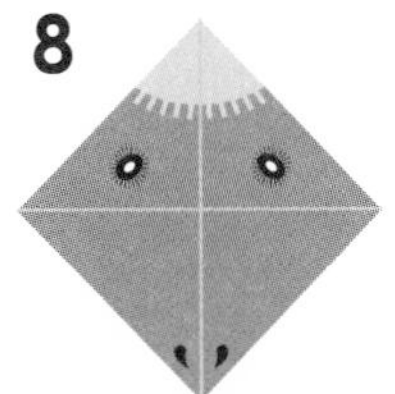

Turn over.

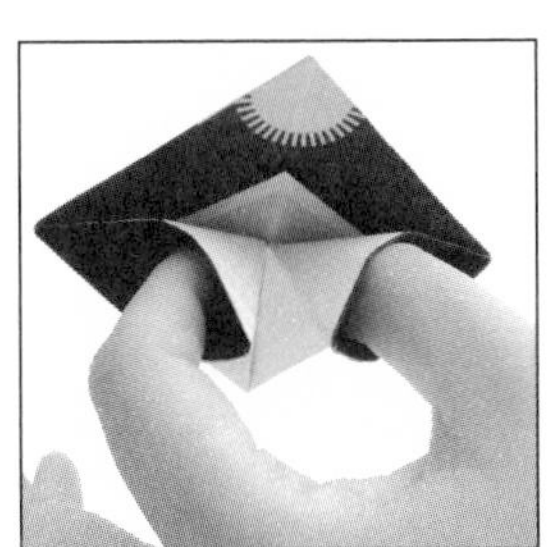

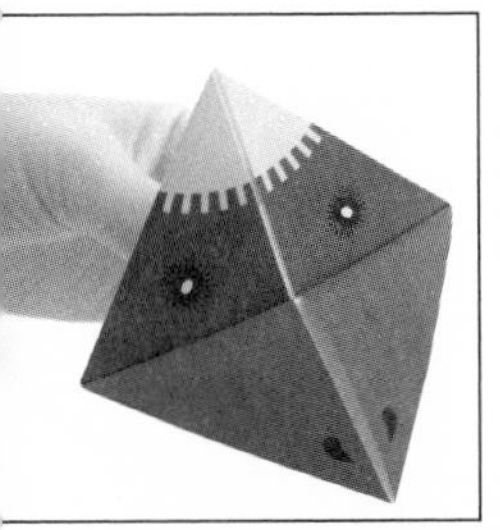

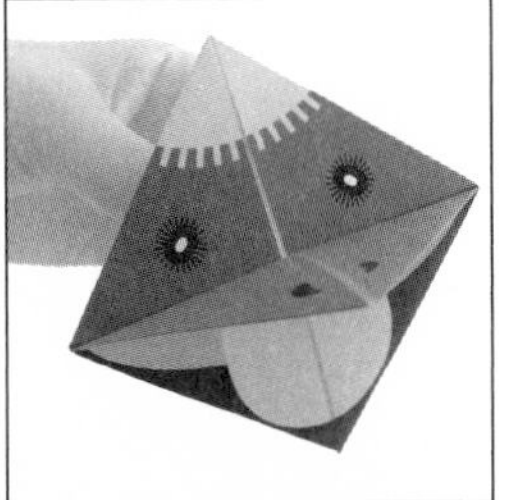

Insert your thumb and index finger as shown and squeeze and spread to make the *kappa* chatter!

TEAR OFF COLORED SHEET ALONG THIS EDGE

サク

FENCE
(Saku)

For high-jumpin' aficionados, the frog (page 73) is a true test of your folding mettle. Will your folds be clean and crisp enough to enable the frog to hop over this "bamboo" fence? Makes a great background too!

TEAR OFF COLORED SHEET ALONG THIS EDGE

Valley fold and stand on a table. Press down on the back of the frog and then snap and release. Can you get the froggie to jump the fence?

クダモノ

FRUIT GIFTIES (Kudamono)

Use scissors to cut out these tasty-looking fruit and place them in your origami gift box. They make great stickers too!

TEAR OFF COLORED SHEET ALONG THIS EDGE

Cut out the fruit with scissors and load them into your basket!

ドヒョウ

SUMO RING *(Dohyo)*

The *dohyo* is where sumo wrestlers battle it out. Place your ring on a flat surface or, better, an empty box and drum or pound on the sides so the wrestlers shimmy and shake about. Will your wrestler be the winner and take home the Emperor's Cup?

TEAR OFF COLORED SHEET ALONG THIS EDGE

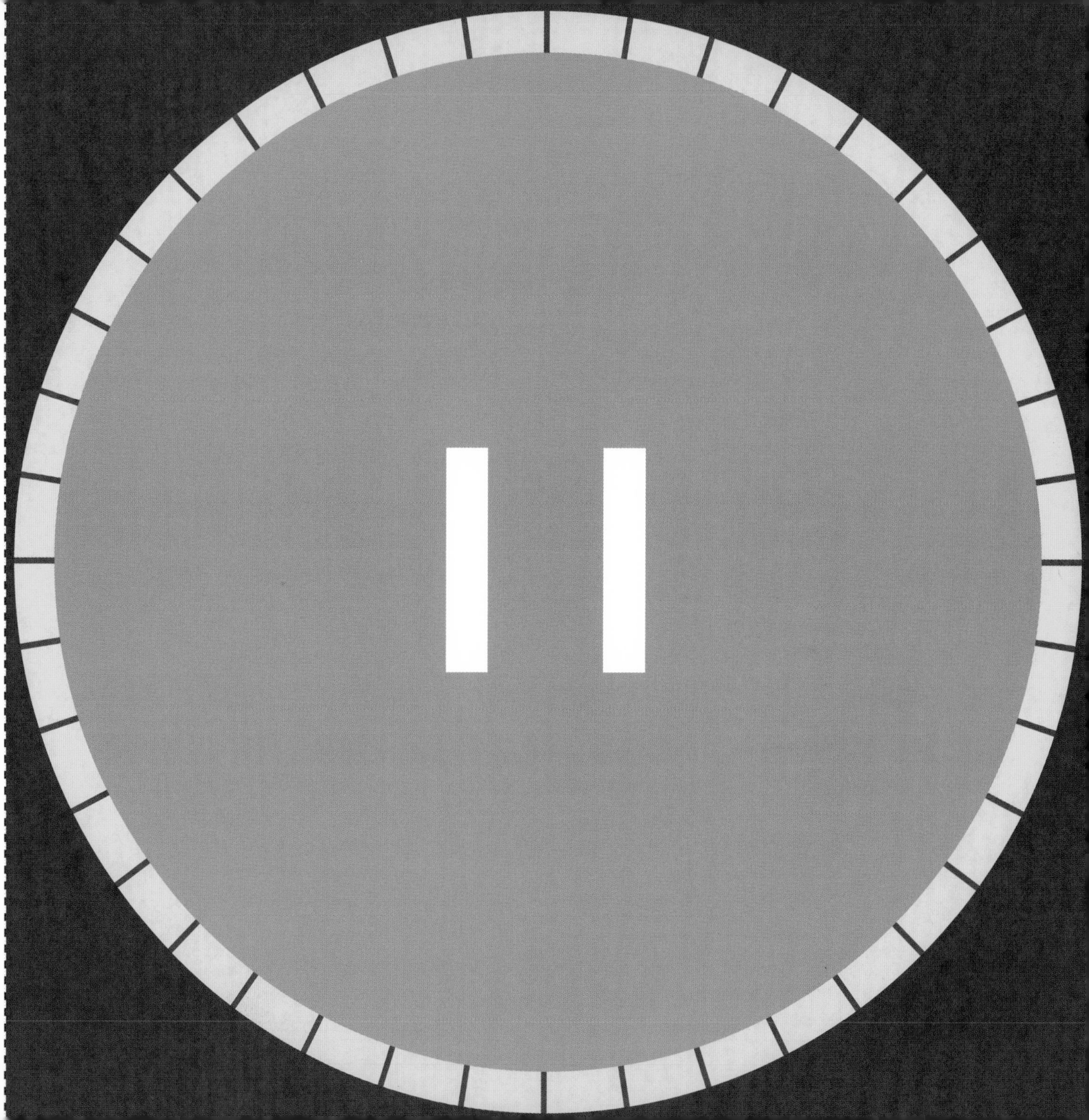

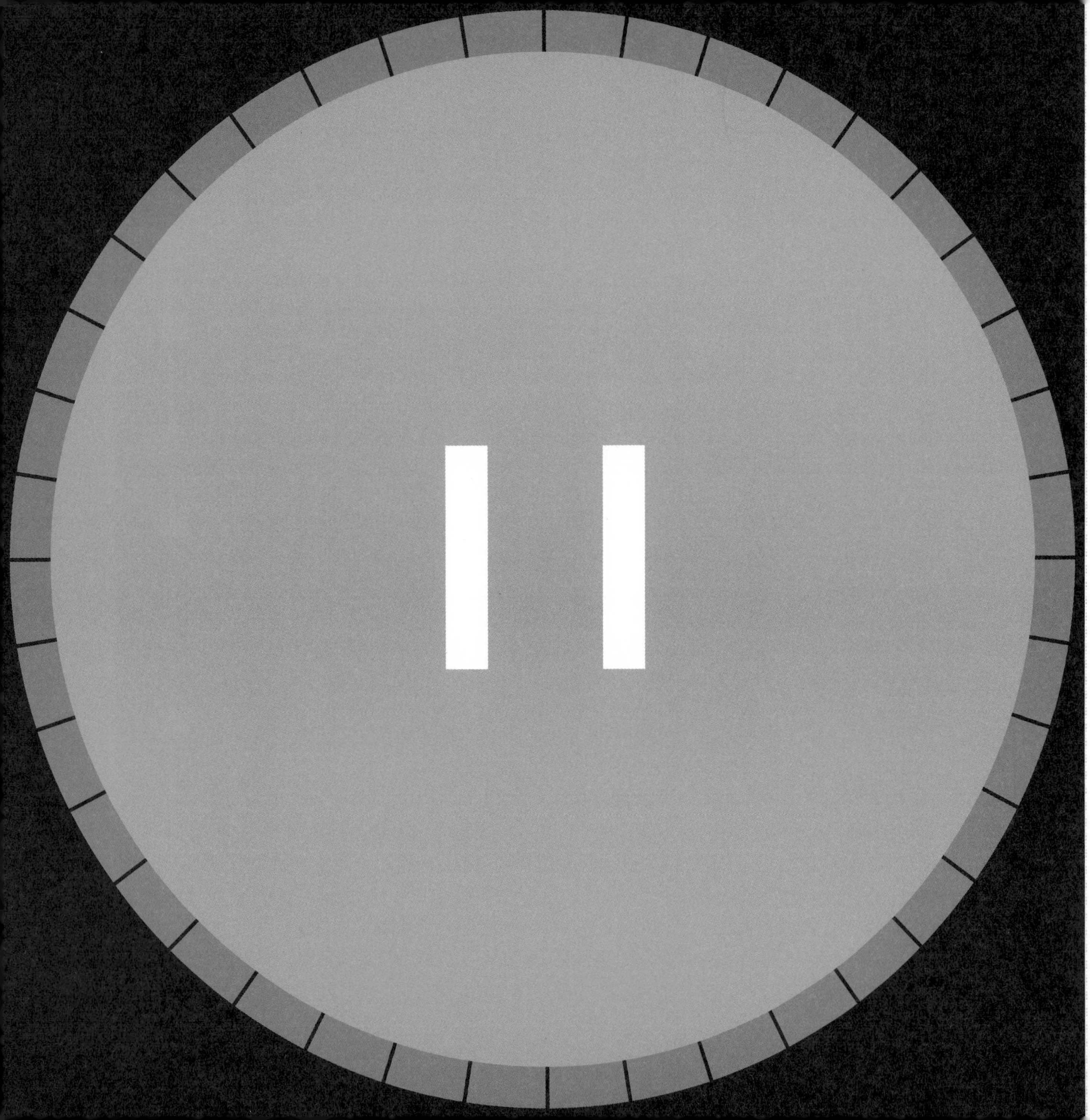

Place atop an empty box and drum with your fingers to move the wrestlers about. The first one to leave the ring or topple over loses!

マト

TARGET
(Mato)

Launch your high-flyin' origami airplane (page 1) and see if you can hit the target. This makes a great party game if you want to avoid sharp-tipped darts. You can also lay the target down flat and aim for it with your leaping frog (page 73).

TEAR OFF COLORED SHEET ALONG THIS EDGE

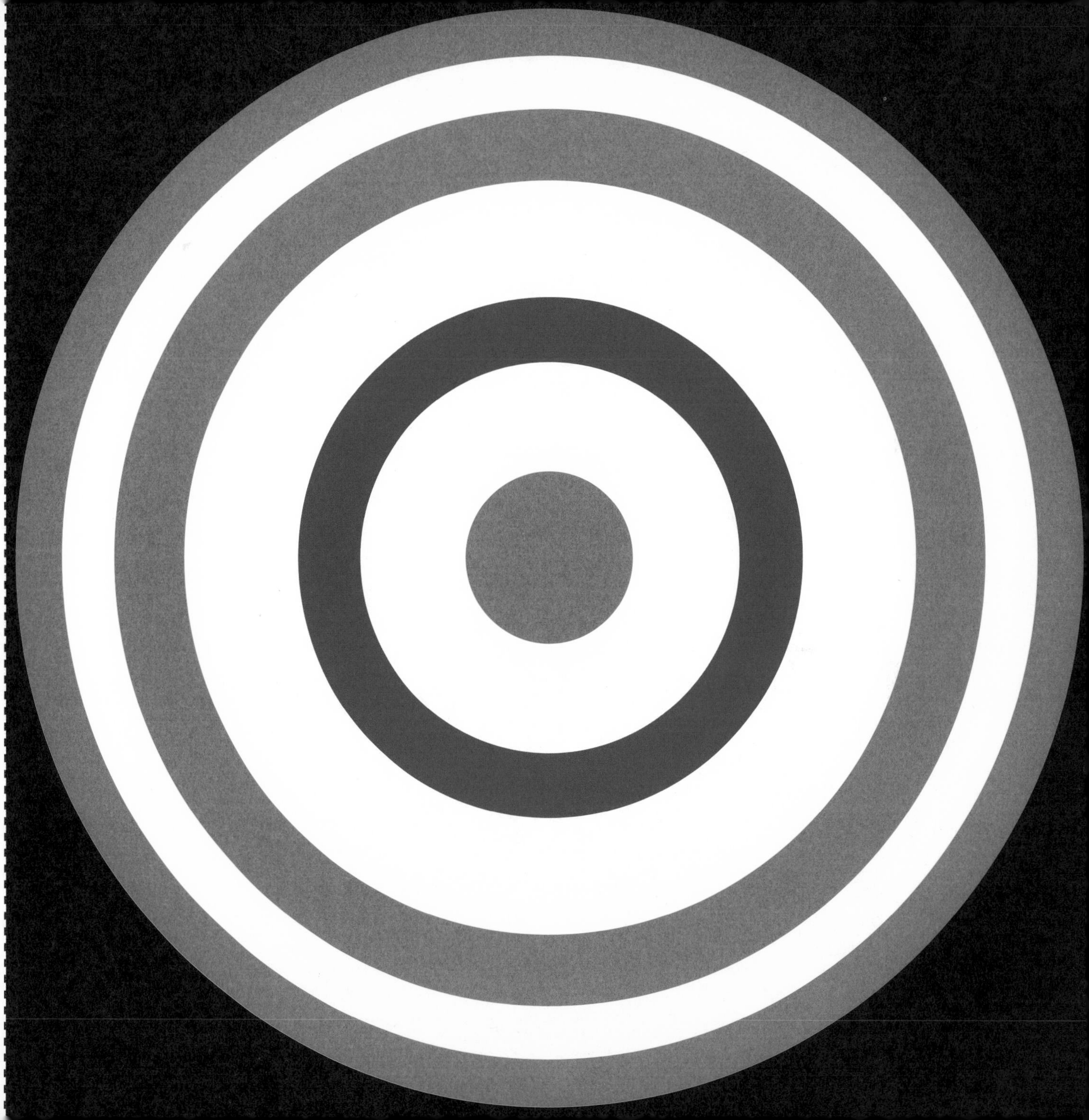

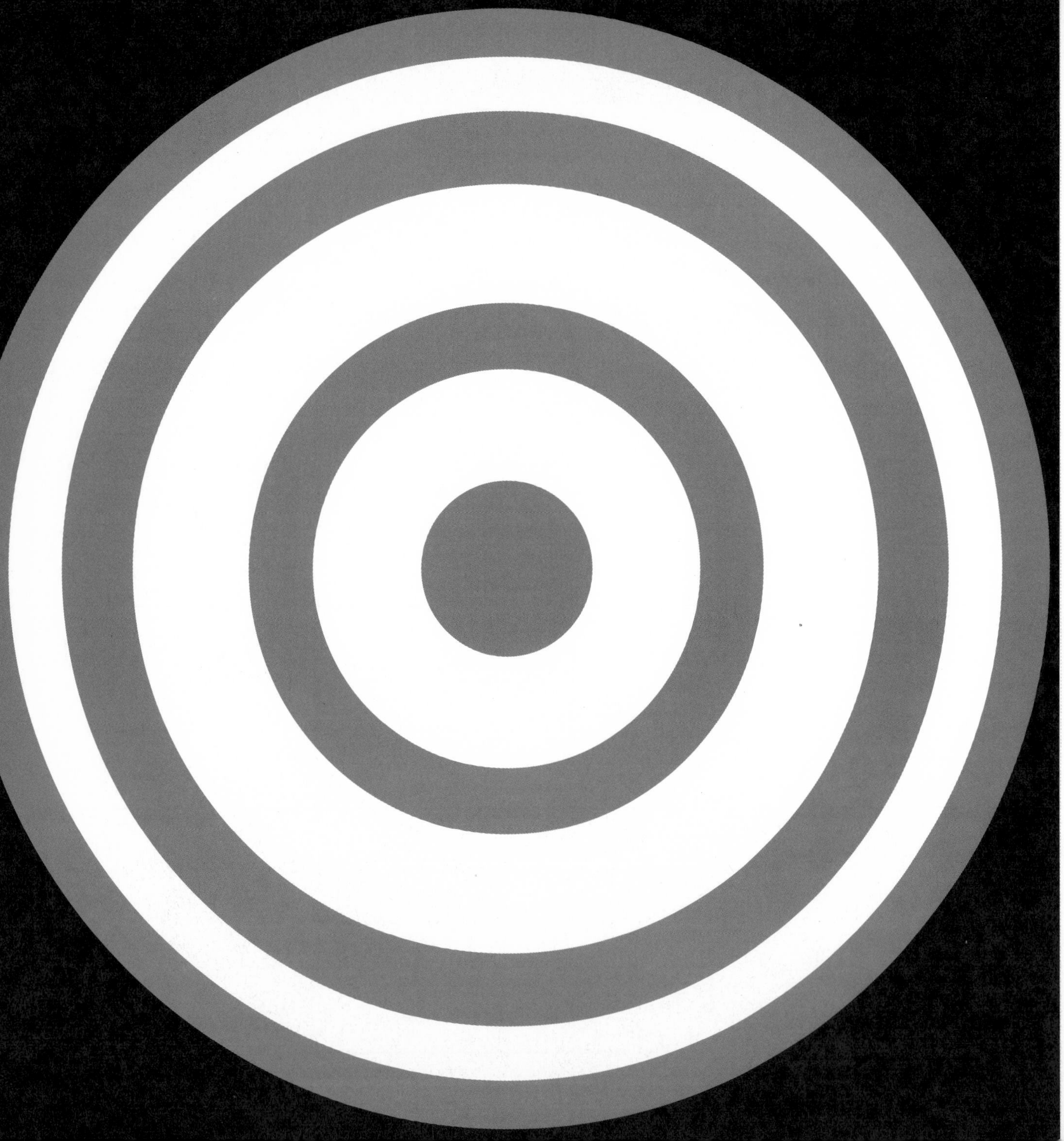

Hold the origami airplane like this and send it flying. Can you hit the target?